Poem

A Classic ᴄᴏ...

Book

Edited by
Debbie Brewer

Cover Portrait by
François D'Albert Durade

ISBN-13: 978-0-244-54755-4

Second Edition

More From The Classic
Collection Range

Poems of Francis Scott Fitzgerald

Poems of Jane Austen

Poems of Anne Bronte

Poems of Charlotte Bronte

Poems of Emily Bronte

Poems of the Bronte Sisters

Poems of Charles Dickens

Poems of Mark Twain

Sonnets of Shakespeare

And more

A
Classic
Collection
Book

Poems of
George
Eliot

Foreword

Mary Ann Evans (1819 - 1880) was an English novelist who wrote under her pen name George Eliot to escape the stereotype of women's writing being limited to light-hearted romances.

She wrote seven novels, including The Mill On The Floss, Middlemarch, and Silas Marner, and she became one of the leading writers of the Victorian era.

As well as her classic novels, she also wrote exceptional poetry which demonstrated her natural talent at writing prose and rhyme that displayed realism and psychological insight.

This comprehensive collection of George Eliots poetry includes Self And Life, Bright, O Bright Fedalma, Brother And Sister, God Needs Antonio, The Choir Invisible, Two Lovers, I Grant You Ample Leave, The Radiant Dark, Blue Wings and many more.

George Eliot Poems

Making Life Worth While

I Am Lonely

Self And Life

Bright, O Bright Fedalma

Spring Comes Hither

Brother and Sister

Sweet Springtime

Blue Wings

Ay De Mi

The World Is Great

The Radiant Dark

Came A Pretty Maid

Day Is Dying

Mid My Gold-Brown Curls

God Needs Antonio (Stradivarius)

Making Life Worth While

Every soul that touches yours -
Be it the slightest contact -
Get there from some good;
Some little grace; one kindly
thought;
One aspiration yet unfelt;
One bit of courage
For the darkening sky;
One gleam of faith
To brave the thickening ills of
life;
One glimpse of brighter skies -
To make this life worthwhile
And heaven a surer heritage.

I Am Lonely

The world is great: the birds all
fly from me,
The stars are golden fruit upon a
tree
All out of reach: my little sister
went,
And I am lonely.

The world is great: I tried to
mount the hill
Above the pines, where the light
lies so still,
But it rose higher: little Lisa
went
And I am lonely.

The world is great: the wind
comes rushing by.
I wonder where it comes from;
sea birds cry
And hurt my heart: my little
sister went,
And I am lonely.

The world is great: the people
laugh and talk,
And make loud holiday: how
fast they walk!
I'm lame, they push me: little
Lisa went,
And I am lonely.

Self And Life

SELF
Changeful comrade, Life of
mine,
Before we two must part,
I will tell thee, thou shalt say,
What thou hast been and art.
Ere I lose my hold of thee
Justify thyself to me.

LIFE
I was thy warmth upon thy
mother's knee
When light and love within her
eyes were one;
We laughed together by the
laurel-tree,
Culling warm daisies 'neath the
sloping sun;
We heard the chickens' lazy
croon,

Where the trellised woodbines
grew,
And all the summer afternoon
Mystic gladness o'er thee threw.
Was it person? Was it thing?
Was it touch or whispering?
It was bliss and it was I:
Bliss was what thou knew'st me
by.

SELF
Soon I knew thee more by Fear
And sense of what was not,
Haunting all I held most dear
I had a double lot:
Ardour, cheated with alloy,
Wept the more for dreams of
joy.

LIFE
Remember how thy ardour's
magic sense
Made poor things rich to thee

and small things great;
How hearth and garden, field
and bushy fence,
Were thy own eager love
incorporate;
And how the solemn, splendid
Past
O'er thy early widened earth
Made grandeur, as on sunset
cast
Dark elms near take mighty
girth.
Hands and feet were tiny still
When we knew the historic
thrill,
Breathed deep breath in heroes
dead,
Tasted the immortals' bread.

SELF
Seeing what I might have been
Reproved the thing I was,
Smoke on heaven's clearest

sheen,
The speck within the rose.
By revered ones' frailties stung
Reverence was with anguish
wrung.

LIFE
But all thy anguish and thy
discontent
Was growth of mine, the
elemental strife
Towards feeling manifold with
vision blent
To wider thought: I was no
vulgar life
That, like the water-mirrored
ape,
Not discerns the thing it sees,
Nor knows its own in others'
shape,
Railing, scorning, at its ease.
Half man's truth must hidden lie
If unlit by Sorrow's eye.

I by Sorrow wrought in thee
Willing pain of ministry.

SELF
Slowly was the lesson taught
Through passion, error, care;
Insight was with loathing
fraught
And effort with despair.
Written on the wall I saw
'Bow!' I knew, not loved, the
law.

LIFE
But then I brought a love that
wrote within
The law of gratitude, and made
thy heart
Beat to the heavenly tune of
seraphin
Whose only joy in having is, to
impart:
Till thou, poor Self — despite

thy ire,
Wrestling 'gainst my mingled
share,
Thy faults, hard falls, and vain
desire
Still to be what others were —
Filled, o'erflowed with
tenderness
Seeming more as thou wert less,
Knew me through that anguish
past
As a fellowship more vast.

SELF
Yea, I embrace thee, changeful
Life!
Far-sent, unchosen mate!
Self and thou, no more at strife,
Shall wed in hallowed state.
Willing spousals now shall prove
Life is justified by love.

Bright, O Bright Fedalma

Maiden crowned with glossy
blackness,
Lithe as panther forest-roaming,
Long-armed Naiad when she
dances
On a stream of ether floating,
Bright, o bright Fedalma!

Form all curves like softness
drifted,
Wave-kissed marble roundly
dimpling,
Far-off music slowly wingèd,
Gently rising, gently sinking,
Bright, o bright Fedalma!

Pure as rain-tear on a rose-leaf,
Cloud high born in noonday
spotless
Sudden perfect like the dew-
bead,
Gem of earth and sky begotten,
Bright, o bright Fedalma!

Beauty has no mortal father,
Holy light her form engendered,
Out of tremor yearning,
gladness,
Presage sweet, and joy
remembered,
Child of light! Child of light!
Child of light, Fedalma!

Spring Comes Hither

Spring comes hither
Buds the rose . . .
Roses wither
Sweet spring goes . . .
O ja là
O ja là . . .
Would she carry me.

Summer soars
Wide-wing'd day . . .
White light pours
Flies away . . .
O ja là
O ja là . . .
Would he carry me.

Soft winds blow
Westward borne . . .
Onward go
Towards the morn
O ja là
O ja là . . .
Would they carry me.

Sweet birds sing
O'er the graves
Then take wing
O'er the waves
O ja là
O ja là . . .
Would they carry me.

Brother and Sister

I.

I cannot choose but think upon
the time
When our two lives grew like
two buds that kiss
At lightest thrill from the bee's
swinging chime,
Because the one so near the
other is.

He was the elder and a little
man
Of forty inches, bound to show
no dread,
And I the girl that puppy-like
now ran,
Now lagged behind my brother's
larger tread.

I held him wise, and when he
talked to me
Of snakes and birds, and which
God loved the best,
I thought his knowledge marked
the boundary
Where men grew blind, though
angels knew the rest.

If he said 'Hush!' I tried to hold
my breath;
Wherever he said 'Come!' I
stepped in faith.

II.

Long years have left their
writing on my brow,
But yet the freshness and the
dew-fed beam
Of those young mornings are
about me now,
When we two wandered toward
the far-off stream

With rod and line. Our basket
held a store
Baked for us only, and I thought
with joy
That I should have my share,
though he had more,
Because he was the elder and a
boy.

The firmaments of daisies since
to me

Have had those mornings in
their opening eyes,
The bunchèd cowslip's pale
transparency
Carries that sunshine of sweet
memories,

And wild-rose branches take
their finest scent
From those blest hours of
infantine content.

III.

Our mother bade us keep the
trodden ways,
Stroked down my tippet, set my
brother's frill,
Then with the benediction of
her gaze
Clung to us lessening, and
pursued us still

Across the homestead to the
rookery elms,
Whose tall old trunks had each a
grassy mound,
So rich for us, we counted them
as realms
With varied products: here were
earth-nuts found,

And here the Lady-fingers in
deep shade;

Here sloping toward the Moat
the rushes grew,
The large to split for pith, the
small to braid;
While over all the dark rooks
cawing flew,

And made a happy strange
solemnity,
A deep-toned chant from life
unknown to me.

IV.

Our meadow-path had
memorable spots:
One where it bridged a tiny
rivulet,
Deep hid by tangled blue
Forget-me-nots;
And all along the waving grasses
met

My little palm, or nodded to my
cheek,
When flowers with upturned
faces gazing drew
My wonder downward, seeming
all to speak
With eyes of souls that dumbly
heard and knew.

Then came the copse, where
wild things rushed unseen,

And black-scathed grass
betrayed the past abode
Of mystic gypsies, who still
lurked between
Me and each hidden distance of
the road.

A gypsy once had startled me at
play,
Blotting with her dark smile my
sunny day.

V.

Thus rambling we were
schooled in deepest lore,
And learned the meanings that
give words a soul,
The fear, the love, the primal
passionate store,
Whose shaping impulses make
manhood whole.

Those hours were seed to all my
after good;
My infant gladness, through
eye, ear, and touch,
Took easily as warmth a various
food
To nourish the sweet skill of
loving much.

For who in age shall roam the
earth and find

Reasons for loving that will
strike out love
With sudden rod from the hard
year-pressed mind?
Were reasons sown as thick as
stars above,

'Tis love must see them, as the
eye sees light:
Day is but Number to the
darkened sight.

VI.

Our brown canal was endless to
my thought;
And on its banks I sat in dreamy
peace,
Unknowing how the good I
loved was wrought,
Untroubled by the fear that it
would cease.

Slowly the barges floated into
view
Rounding a grassy hill to me
sublime
With some Unknown beyond it,
whither flew
The parting cuckoo toward a
fresh spring time.

The wide-arched bridge, the
scented elder-flowers,

The wondrous watery rings that
died too soon,
The echoes of the quarry, the
still hours
With white robe sweeping-on
the shadeless noon,

Were but my growing self, are
part of me,
My present Past, my root of
piety.

VII.

Those long days measured by
my little feet
Had chronicles which yield me
many a text;
Where irony still finds an image
meet
Of full-grown judgments in this
world perplext.

One day my brother left me in
high charge,
To mind the rod, while he went
seeking bait,
And bade me, when I saw a
nearing barge,
Snatch out the line lest he
should come too late.

Proud of the task, I watched
with all my might

For one whole minute, till my
eyes grew wide,
Till sky and earth took on a
strange new light
And seemed a dream-world
floating on some tide -

A fair pavilioned boat for me
alone
Bearing me onward through the
vast unknown.

VIII.

But sudden came the barge's
pitch-black prow,
Nearer and angrier came my
brother's cry,
And all my soul was quivering
fear, when lo!
Upon the imperilled line,
suspended high,

A silver perch! My guilt that won
the prey,
Now turned to merit, had a
guerdon rich
Of songs and praises, and made
merry play,
Until my triumph reached its
highest pitch

When all at home were told the
wondrous feat,

And how the little sister had
fished well.
In secret, though my fortune
tasted sweet,
I wondered why this happiness
befell.

'The little lass had luck,' the
gardener said:
And so I learned, luck was with
glory wed.

IX.

We had the self-same world
enlarged for each
By loving difference of girl and
boy:
The fruit that hung on high
beyond my reach
He plucked for me, and oft he
must employ

A measuring glance to guide my
tiny shoe
Where lay firm stepping-stones,
or call to mind
'This thing I like my sister may
not do,
For she is little, and I must be
kind.'

Thus boyish Will the nobler
mastery learned

Where inward vision over
impulse reigns,
Widening its life with separate
life discerned,
A Like unlike, a Self that self-
restrains.

His years with others must the
sweeter be
For those brief days he spent in
loving me.

X.

His sorrow was my sorrow, and
his joy
Sent little leaps and laughs
through all my frame;
My doll seemed lifeless and no
girlish toy
Had any reason when my
brother came.

I knelt with him at marbles,
marked his fling
Cut the ringed stem and make
the apple drop,
Or watched him winding close
the spiral string
That looped the orbits of the
humming top.

Grasped by such fellowship my
vagrant thought

Ceased with dream-fruit dream-
wishes to fulfil;
My aëry-picturing fantasy was
taught
Subjection to the harder, truer
skill

That seeks with deeds to grave a
thought-tracked line,
And by 'What is,' 'What will be'
to define.

XI.

School parted us; we never found again
That childish world where our two spirits mingled
Like scents from varying roses that remain
One sweetness, nor can evermore be singled.

Yet the twin habit of that early time
Lingered for long about the heart and tongue:
We had been natives of one happy clime
And its dear accent to our utterance clung.

Till the dire years whose awful name is Change

Had grasped our souls still
yearning in divorce,
And pitiless shaped them in two
forms that range
Two elements which sever their
life's course.

But were another childhood-
world my share,
I would be born a little sister
there.

Sweet Springtime

It was in the prime
Of the sweet springtime
In the linnet's throat
Trembled the love note,
And the love-stirred air
Thrilled the blossoms there.
Little shadows danced,
Each a tiny elf
Happy in large light
And the thinnest self.

It was but a minute
In a far-off spring,
But each gentle thing,
Sweetly wooing linnet,
Soft thrilled hawthorn tree,
Happy shadowy elf,
With the thinnest self,
Live on still in me.
It was in the prime
Of the past springtime!

Blue Wings

Warm whisp'ring through the
slender olive leaves
Came to me a gentle sound,
Whis'pring of a secret found
In the clear sunshine 'mid the
golden sheaves:

Said it was sleeping for me in
the morn,
Called it gladness, called it joy,
Drew me on 'Come hither, boy.'
To where the blue wings rested
on the corn.

I thought the gentle sound had
whispered true
Thought the little heaven mine,
Leaned to clutch the thing
divine,
And saw the blue wings melt
within the blue!

Ay De Mi

O bird, that used to press,
Thy head against my cheek
With touch that seem'd to
speak,
And ask a tender 'yes' -
Ay de mi, my bird:
Ay de mi, my bird, my bird -
Ay de mi, my bird.

O tender downy breast,
And warmly beating heart,
That beating seem'd a part
Of me who gave it rest -
Ay de mi, my bird:
Ay de mi, my bird, my bird -
Ay de mi, my bird.

The World Is Great

The world is great!
The birds fly from me;
The stars are golden fruit
Upon a tree
All out of reach
My little sister went and I am
lonely.

The world is great!
I tried to mount the hill
Above the pines
Where the light lies so still,
But it rose higher.
Little Lisa went and I am lonely.

The world is great!
The wind comes rushing by.
I wonder where it comes from.
Sea-birds cry
And hurt my heart.
My little sister went and I am
lonely.

The world is great!
The people laugh and talk,
And make loud holiday.
How fast they walk!
I'm lame, they push me.
Little Lisa went and I am lonely.

The Radiant Dark

Should I long that dark were
fair? Say, O song.
Lacks my love aught that I
should long?
Dark the night with breath all
flow'rs
And tender broken voice that
fills
With ravishment the list'ning
hours.
Whis'prings, wooings,
Liquid ripples, and soft ring-
dove cooings,
in low-toned rhythm that love's
aching stills.

Dark the night, yet is she bright,
For in her dark she brings the
mystic star,
Trembling yet strong as is the
voice of love
From some unknown afar.
O radiant dark, O darkly foster'd
ray,
Thou hast a joy too deep for
shallow day.

Came A Pretty Maid

Came a pretty maid
By the moon's pure light . . .
Loved me well, she said,
Eyes with tears all bright,
A pretty maid.

But too late she strayed,
Moonlight pure was there . . .
She was nought but shade,
Hiding the more fair,
The heav'nly maid.

Day Is Dying

Day is dying! Float, o song,
Down the westward river,
Requiem chanting to the Day,
Day, the mighty giver!

Pierced by shafts of Time he
bleeds,
Melted rubies sending
Through the river and the sky,
Earth and heaven blending.

All the long-drawn earthy banks
Up to cloudland lifting:
Slow between them drifts the
swan
'Twixt two heavens drifting,

Wings half open like a flower.
In by deeper flushing,
Neck and breast as virgin's pure
Virgin proudly blushing.

Day is dying! Float, o swan,
Down the ruby river,
Follow, song, in requiem
To the mighty Giver!

Mid My Gold-Brown Curls

'Mid my gold-brown curls
There twined a silver hair:
I plucked it idly out
And scarcely knew 'twas there.
Coiled in my velvet sleeve it lay
And like a serpent hissed:
"Me thou canst pluck & fling
away,
One hair is lightly missed;
But how on that near day
When all the wintry army
muster in array?"

God Needs Antonio
(Stradivarius)

Your soul was lifted by the
wings today
Hearing the master of the violin:
You praised him, praised the
great Sabastian too
Who made that fine Chaconne;
but did you think
Of old Antonio Stradivari? -him
Who a good century and a half
ago
Put his true work in that brown
instrument
And by the nice adjustment of
its frame
Gave it responsive life,
continuous
With the master's finger-tips
and perfected
Like them by delicate rectitude

of use.
That plain white-aproned man,
who stood at work
Patient and accurate full
fourscore years,
Cherished his sight and touch by
temperance,
And since keen sense is love of
perfectness
Made perfect violins, the
needed paths
For inspiration and high
mastery.

No simpler man than he; he
never cried,
"why was I born to this
monotonous task
Of making violins?" or flung
them down
To suit with hurling act well-
hurled curse
At labor on such perishable

stuff.
Hence neighbors in Cremona
held him dull,
Called him a slave, a mill-horse,
a machine.

Naldo, a painter of eclectic
school,
Knowing all tricks of style at
thirty-one,
And weary of them, while
Antonio
At sixty-nine wrought placidly
his best,
Making the violin you heard
today -
Naldo would tease him oft to
tell his aims.
"Perhaps thou hast some
pleasant vice to feed -
the love of louis d'ors in heaps
of four,
Each violin a heap - I've naught

to blame;
My vices waste such heaps. But
then, why work
With painful nicety?"

Antonio then:
"I like the gold - well, yes - but
not for meals.
And as my stomach, so my eye
and hand,
And inward sense that works
along with both,
Have hunger that can never
feed on coin.
Who draws a line and satisfies
his soul,
Making it crooked where it
should be straight?
Antonio Stradivari has an eye
That winces at false work and
loves the true."
Then Naldo: "'Tis a petty kind of
fame

At best, that comes of making
violins;
And saves no masses, either.
Thou wilt go
To purgatory none the less."

But he:
"'Twere purgatory here to make
them ill;
And for my fame - when any
master holds
'Twixt chin and hand a violin of
mine,
He will be glad that Stradivari
lived,
Made violins, and made them of
the best.
The masters only know whose
work is good:
They will choose mine, and
while God gives them skill
I give them instruments to play
upon,

God choosing me to help him.

"What! Were God
at fault for violins, thou
absent?"

"Yes;
He were at fault for Stradivari's
work."

"Why, many hold Giuseppe's
violins
As good as thine."

"May be: they are different.
His quality declines: he spoils his
hand
With over-drinking. But were his
the best,
He could not work for two. My
work is mine,
And, heresy or not, if my hand
slacked

I should rob God - since his is
fullest good -
Leaving a blank instead of
violins.
I say, not God himself can make
man's best
Without best men to help him.

'Tis God gives skill,
But not without men's hands:
he could not make
Antonio Stradivari's violins
Without Antonio. Get thee to
thy easel."

I Grant You Ample Leave

"I grant you ample leave
To use the hoary formula 'I am'
Naming the emptiness where
thought is not;
But fill the void with definition,
'I'
Will be no more a datum than
the words
You link false inference with, the
'Since' & 'so'
That, true or not, make up the
atom-whirl.
Resolve your 'Ego', it is all one
web
With vibrant ether clotted into
worlds:
Your subject, self, or self-
assertive 'I'
Turns nought but object, melts
to molecules,

Is stripped from naked Being
with the rest
Of those rag-garments named
the Universe.
Or if, in strife to keep your 'Ego'
strong
You make it weaver of the
etherial light,
Space, motion, solids & the
dream of Time --
Why, still 'tis Being looking from
the dark,
The core, the centre of your
consciousness,
That notes your bubble-world:
sense, pleasure, pain,
What are they but a shifting
otherness,
Phantasmal flux of moments? –"

The Choir Invisible

Oh, may I join the choir invisible
Of those immortal dead who
live again
In minds made better by their
presence; live
In pulses stirred to generosity,
In deeds of daring rectitude, in
scorn
For miserable aims that end
with self,
In thoughts sublime that pierce
the night like stars,
And with their mild persistence
urge men's search
To vaster issues. So to live is
heaven:
To make undying music in the
world,
Breathing a beauteous order
that controls

With growing sway the growing
life of man.
So we inherit that sweet purity
For which we struggled, failed,
and agonized
With widening retrospect that
bred despair.
Rebellious flesh that would not
be subdued,
A vicious parent shaming still its
child,
Poor anxious penitence, is quick
dissolved;
Its discords, quenched by
meeting harmonies,
Die in the large and charitable
air,
And all our rarer, better, truer
self
That sobbed religiously in
yearning song,
That watched to ease the
burden of the world,

Laboriously tracing what must
be,
And what may yet be better, --
saw within
A worthier image for the
sanctuary,
And shaped it forth before the
multitude,
Divinely human, raising worship
so
To higher reverence more mixed
with love, --
That better self shall live till
human Time
Shall fold its eyelids, and the
human sky
Be gathered like a scroll within
the tomb
Unread forever. This is life to
come, --
Which martyred men have
made more glorious
For us who strive to follow. May

I reach
That purest heaven, -- be to
other souls
The cup of strength in some
great agony,
Enkindle generous ardour, feed
pure love,
Beget the smiles that have no
cruelty,
Be the sweet presence of a good
diffused,
And in diffusion ever more
intense!
So shall I join the choir invisible
Whose music is the gladness of
the world.

Two Lovers

Two lovers by a moss-grown
spring:
They leaned soft cheeks
together there,
Mingled the dark and sunny
hair,
And heard the wooing thrushes
sing.
O budding time!
O love's blest prime!

Two wedded from the portal
stept:
The bells made happy carolings,
The air was soft as fanning
wings,
White petals on the pathway
slept.
O pure-eyed bride!
O tender pride!

Two faces o'er a cradle bent:
Two hands above the head were
locked:
These pressed each other while
they rocked,
Those watched a life that love
had sent.
O solemn hour!
O hidden power!

Two parents by the evening fire:
The red light fell about their
knees
On heads that rose by slow
degrees
Like buds upon the lily spire.
O patient life!
O tender strife!

The two still sat together there,
The red light shone about their
knees;
But all the heads by slow
degrees
Had gone and left that lonely
pair.
O voyage fast!
O vanished past!

The red light shone upon the
floor
And made the space between
them wide;
They drew their chairs up side
by side,
Their pale cheeks joined, and
said, "Once more!"
O memories!
O past that is!

Sweet Endings Come And Go, Love

"La noche buena se viene,
La noche buena se va,
Y nosotros nos iremos
Y no volveremos mas."
-- Old Villancico.

Sweet evenings come and go,
love,
They came and went of yore:
This evening of our life, love,
Shall go and come no more.

When we have passed away,
love,
All things will keep their name;
But yet no life on earth, love,
With ours will be the same.

The daisies will be there, love,
The stars in heaven will shine:
I shall not feel thy wish, love,
Nor thou my hand in thine.

A better time will come, love,
And better souls be born:
I would not be the best, love,
To leave thee now forlorn.

Roses

You love the roses - so do I. I
wish
The sky would rain down roses,
as they rain
From off the shaken bush. Why
will it not?
Then all the valley would be
pink and white
And soft to tread on. They
would fall as light
As feathers, smelling sweet; and
it would be
Like sleeping and like waking, all
at once!

In A London Drawing Room

The sky is cloudy, yellowed by
the smoke.
For view there are the houses
opposite
Cutting the sky with one long
line of wall
Like solid fog: far as the eye can
stretch
Monotony of surface & of form
Without a break to hang a guess
upon.
No bird can make a shadow as it
flies,
For all is shadow, as in ways
o'erhung
By thickest canvass, where the
golden rays
Are clothed in hemp. No figure
lingering
Pauses to feed the hunger of

the eye
Or rest a little on the lap of life.
All hurry on & look upon the
ground,
Or glance unmarking at the
passers by
The wheels are hurrying too,
cabs, carriages
All closed, in multiplied identity.
The world seems one huge
prison-house & court
Where men are punished at the
slightest cost,
With lowest rate of colour,
warmth & joy.

Count That Day Lost

If you sit down at set of sun
And count the acts that you
have done,
And, counting, find
One self-denying deed, one
word
That eased the heart of him who
heard,
One glance most kind
That fell like sunshine where it
went --
Then you may count that day
well spent.

But if, through all the livelong day,
You've cheered no heart, by yea or nay --
If, through it all
You've nothing done that you can trace
That brought the sunshine to one face--
No act most small
That helped some soul and nothing cost --
Then count that day as worse than lost.

Sonnet

Oft, when a child, while
wand'ring far alone,
That none might rouse me from
my waking dream,
And visions with which fancy
still would teem
Scare by a disenchanting earthly
tone;
If, haply, conscious of the
present scene,
I've marked before me some
untraversed spot
The setting sunbeams had
forsaken not,
Whose turf appeared more
velvet-like and green
Than that I walked and fitter for
repose:
But ever, at the wished-for place
arrived,

I've found it of those seeming
charms deprived
Which from the mellowing
power of distance rose:
To my poor thought, an apt
though simple trope
Of life's dull path and earth's
deceitful hope.

How Lisa Loved The King

Six hundred years ago, in
Dante's time,
Before his cheek was furrowed
by deep rhyme;
When Europe, fed afresh from
Eastern story,
Was like a garden tangled with
the glory
Of flowers hand-planted and of
flowers air-sown,
Climbing and trailing, budding
and full-blown,
Where purple bells are tossed
amid pink stars,
And springing blades, green
troops in innocent wars,
Crowd every shady spot of
teeming earth,
Making invisible motion visible
birth,--

Six hundred years ago, Palermo
town
Kept holiday. A deed of great
renown,
A high revenge, had freed it
from the yoke
Of hated Frenchmen; and from
Calpe's rock
To where the Bosporus caught
the earlier sun,
'Twas told that Pedro, King of
Aragon,
Was welcomed master of all
Sicily,--
A royal knight, supreme as kings
should be
In strength and gentleness that
make high chivalry.

Spain was the favourite home of
knightly grace,
Where generous men rode

steeds of generous race;
Both Spanish, yet half Arab;
both inspired
By mutual spirit, that each
motion fired
With beauteous response, like
minstrelsy
Afresh fulfilling fresh
expectancy.
So, when Palermo made high
festival,
The joy of matrons and of
maidens all
Was the mock terror of the
tournament,
Where safety, with the glimpse
of danger blent,
Took exaltation as from epic
song,
Which greatly tells the pains
that to great life belong.

And in all eyes King Pedro was

the king
Of cavaliers; as in a full-gemmed
ring
The largest ruby, or as that
bright star
Whose shining shows us where
the Hyads are.
His the best genet, and he sat it
best;
His weapon, whether tilting or
in rest,
Was worthiest watching; and his
face, once seen,
Gave to the promise of his royal
mien
Such rich fulfilment as the
opened eyes
Of a loved sleeper, or the long-
watched rise
Of vernal day, whose joy o'er
stream and meadow flies.

But of the maiden forms that

thick enwreathed
The broad piazza, and sweet
witchery breathed,
With innocent faces budding all
arow,
From balconies and windows
high and low,
Who was it felt the deep
mysterious glow,
The impregnation with supernal
fire
Of young ideal love,
transformed desire,
Whose passion is but worship of
that Best
Taught by the many-mingled
creed of each young breast?

'Twas gentle Lisa, of no noble
line,
Child of Bernardo, a rich
Florentine,
Who from his merchant-city

hither came
To trade in drugs; yet kept an
honest fame,
And had the virtue not to try
and sell
Drugs that had none. He loved
his riches well,
But loved them chiefly for his
Lisa's sake,
Whom with a father's care he
sought to make
The bride of some true
honourable man,--
Of Perdicone (so the rumour
ran),
Whose birth was higher than his
fortunes were,
For still your trader likes a
mixture fair
Of blood that hurries to some
higher strain
Than reckoning money's loss
and money's gain.

And of such mixture good may
surely come:
Lord's scions so may learn to
cast a sum,
A trader's grandson bear a well-
set head,
And have less conscious
manners, better bred;
Nor, when he tries to be polite,
be rude instead.

'Twas Perdicone's friends made
overtures
To good Bernardo; so one dame
assures
Her neighbour dame, who
notices the youth
Fixing his eyes on Lisa; and, in
truth,
Eyes that could see her on this
summer day
Might find it hard to turn
another way.

She had a pensive beauty, yet
not sad;
Rather like minor cadences that
glad
The hearts of little birds amid
spring boughs:
And oft the trumpet or the joust
would rouse
Pulses that gave her cheek a
finer glow,
Parting her lips that seemed a
mimic bow
By chiselling Love for play in
coral wrought,
Then quickened by him with the
passionate thought,
The soul that trembled in the
lustrous night
Of slow long eyes. Her body was
so slight,
It seemed she could have
floated in the sky,
And with the angelic choir made

symphony;
But in her cheek's rich tinge, and
in the dark
Of darkest hair and eyes, she
bore a mark
Of kinship to her generous
mother-earth,
The fervid land that gives the
plumy palm-trees birth.

She saw not Perdicone; her
young mind
Dreamed not that any man had
ever pined
For such a little simple maid as
she:
She had but dreamed how
heavenly it would be
To love some hero noble,
beauteous, great,
Who would live stories worthy
to narrate,
Like Roland, or the warriors of

Troy,
The Cid, or Amadis, or that fair
boy
Who conquered everything
beneath the sun,
And somehow, some time, died
at Babylon
Fighting the Moors. For heroes
all were good
And fair as that archangel who
withstood
The Evil One, the author of all
wrong,--
That Evil One who made the
French so strong;
And now the flower of heroes
must he be
Who drove those tyrants from
dear Sicily,
So that her maids might walk to
vespers tranquilly.

Young Lisa saw this hero in the

king;
And as wood-lilies that sweet
odours bring
Might dream the light that opes
their modest eyne
Was lily-odoured; and as rites
divine,
Round turf-laid altars, or 'neath
roofs of stone,
Draw sanctity from out the
heart alone
That loves and worships: so the
miniature
Perplexed of her soul's world, all
virgin pure,
Filled with heroic virtues that
bright form,
Raona's royalty, the finished
norm
Of horsemanship, the half of
chivalry;
For how could generous men
avengers be,

Save as God's messengers on
coursers fleet?--
These, scouring earth, made
Spain with Syria meet
In one self-world where the
same right had sway,
And good must grow as grew
the blessed day.
No more: great Love his essence
had endued
With Pedro's form, and,
entering, subdued
The soul of Lisa, fervid and
intense,
Proud in its choice of proud
obedience
To hardship glorified by perfect
reverence.

Sweet Lisa homeward carried
that dire guest,
And in her chamber, through
the hours of rest,

The darkness was alight for her
with sheen
Of arms, and plumed helm; and
bright between
Their commoner gloss, like the
pure living spring
'Twixt porphyry lips, or living
bird's bright wing
'Twixt golden wires, the glances
of the king
Flashed on her soul, and waked
vibrations there
Of known delights love-mixed to
new and rare:
The impalpable dream was
turned to breathing flesh,
Chill thought of summer to the
warm close mesh
Of sunbeams held between the
citron-leaves,
Clothing her life of life. Oh! she
believes
That she could be content if he

but knew
(Her poor small self could claim
no other due)
How Lisa's lowly love had
highest reach
Of winged passion, whereto
winged speech
Would be scorched remnants
left by mounting flame.
Though, had she such lame
message, were it blame
To tell what greatness dwelt in
her, what rank
She held in loving? Modest
maidens shrank
From telling love that fed on
selfish hope;
But love, as hopeless as the
shattering song,
Wailed for loved beings who
have joined the throng
Of mighty dead ones. . . . Nay,
but she was weak,

Knew only prayers and ballads,
could not speak
With eloquence, save what
dumb creatures have,
That with small cries and
touches small boons crave.

She watched all day that she
might see him pass
With knights and ladies; but she
said, "Alas!
Though he should see me, it
were all as one
He saw a pigeon sitting on the
stone
Of wall or balcony: some
coloured spot
His eye just sees, his mind
regardeth not.
I have no music-touch that
could bring nigh
My love to his soul's hearing. I
shall die,

And he will never know who Lisa
was,--
The trader's child, whose
soaring spirit rose
As hedge-born aloe-flowers that
rarest years disclose.

"For were I now a fair deep-
breasted queen
A-horseback, with blonde hair,
and tunic green,
Gold-bordered, like Costanza, I
should need
No change within to make me
queenly there:
For they the royal-hearted
women are
Who nobly love the noblest, yet
have grace;
For needy suffering lives in
lowliest place,
Carrying a choicer sunlight in
their smile,

The heavenliest ray that pitieth
the vile.
My love is such, it cannot
choose but soar
Up to the highest; yet
forevermore,
Though I were happy, throned
beside the king,
I should be tender to each little
thing
With hurt warm breast, that had
no speech to tell
Its inward pang; and I would
soothe it well
With tender touch, and with a
low soft moan
For company: my dumb love-
pang is lone,
Prisoned as topaz-beam within a
rough-garbed stone."

So, inward-wailing, Lisa passed
her days.

Each night the August moon
with changing phase
Looked broader, harder, on her
unchanged pain;
Each noon the heat lay heavier
again
On her despair, until her body
frail
Shrank like the snow that
watchers in the vale
See narrowed on the height
each summer morn;
While her dark glance burnt
larger, more forlorn,
As if the soul within her, all on
fire,
Made of her being one swift
funeral-pyre.
Father and mother saw with sad
dismay
The meaning of their riches melt
away;
For without Lisa what would

sequins buy?
What wish were left if Lisa were
to die?
Through her they cared for
summers still to come,
Else they would be as ghosts
without a home
In any flesh that could feel glad
desire.
They pay the best physicians,
never tire
Of seeking what will soothe her,
promising
That aught she longed for,
though it were a thing
Hard to be come at as the Indian
snow,
Or roses that on Alpine summits
blow,
It should be hers. She answers
with low voice,
She longs for death alone--
death is her choice;

Death is the king who never did
think scorn,
But rescues every meanest soul
to sorrow born.

Yet one day, as they bent above
her bed,
And watched her in brief sleep,
her drooping head
Turned gently, as the thirsty
flowers that feel
Some moist revival through
their petals steal;
And little flutterings of her lids
and lips
Told of such dreamy joy as
sometimes dips
A skyey shadow in the mind's
poor pool.
She oped her eyes, and turned
their dark gems full
Upon her father, as in utterance
dumb

Of some new prayer that in her
sleep had come.
"What is it, Lisa?"--"Father, I
would see
Minuccio, the great singer; bring
him me."
For always, night and day, her
unstilled thought,
Wandering all o'er its little
world, had sought
How she could reach, by some
soft pleading touch,
King Pedro's soul, that she who
loved so much,
Dying, might have a place within
his mind,--
A little grave which he would
sometimes find
And plant some flower on it,--
some thought, some memory
kind.

Till in her dream she saw

Minuccio
Touching his viola, and chanting
low
A strain, that, falling on her
brokenly,
Seemed blossoms lightly blown
from off a tree;
Each burthened with a word
that was a scent,--
Raona, Lisa, love, death,
tournament;
Then in her dream she said, "He
sings of me,
Might be my messenger; ah!
now I see
The king is listening"--Then she
awoke,
And, missing her dear dream,
that new-born longing spoke.
She longed for music: that was
natural;
Physicians said it was medicinal;
The humors might be schooled

by true consent
Of a fine tenor and fine
instrument;
In short, good music, mixed with
doctor's stuff,
Apollo with Asklepios--enough!
Minuccio, entreated, gladly
came.
(He was a singer of most gentle
fame,
A noble, kindly spirit, not elate
That he was famous, but that
song was great;
Would sing as finely to this
suffering child
As at the court where princes on
him smiled.)
Gently he entered and sat down
by her,
Asking what sort of strain she
would prefer,--
The voice alone, or voice with
viol wed;

Then, when she chose the last,
he preluded
With magic hand, that
summoned from the strings
Aerial spirits, rare yet palpable
wings
That fanned the pulses of his
listener,
And waked each sleeping sense
with blissful stir.
Her cheek already showed a
slow, faint blush;
But soon the voice, in pure, full,
liquid rush,
Made all the passion, that till
now she felt,
Seem but as cooler waters that
in warmer melt.

Finished the song, she prayed to
be alone
With kind Minuccio; for her faith
had grown

To trust him as if missioned like
a priest
With some high grace, that,
when his singing ceased,
Still made him wiser, more
magnanimous,
Than common men who had no
genius.
So, laying her small hand within
his palm,
She told him how that secret,
glorious harm
Of loftiest loving had befallen
her;
That death, her only hope, most
bitter were,
If, when she died, her love must
perish too
As songs unsung, and thoughts
unspoken do,
Which else might live within
another breast.
She said, "Minuccio, the grave

were rest,
If I were sure, that, lying cold
and lone,
My love, my best of life, had
safely flown
And nestled in the bosom of the
king.
See, 'tis a small weak bird, with
unfledged wing;
But you will carry it for me
secretly,
And bear it to the king; then
come to me
And tell me it is safe, and I shall
go
Content, knowing that he I love
my love doth know."

Then she wept silently; but each
large tear
Made pleading music to the
inward ear
Of good Minuccio. "Lisa, trust in

me,"
He said, and kissed her fingers
loyally:
"It is sweet law to me to do your
will,
And, ere the sun his round shall
thrice fulfil,
I hope to bring you news of such
rare skill
As amulets have, that aches in
trusting bosoms still."

He needed not to pause and
first devise
How he should tell the king; for
in nowise
Were such love-message
worthily bested
Save in fine verse by music
rendered.
He sought a poet-friend, a
Siennese,
And "Mico, mine," he said, "full

oft to please
Thy whim of sadness I have sung
thee strains
To make thee weep in verse:
now pay my pains,
And write me a canzon divinely
sad,
Sinlessly passionate, and meekly
mad
With young despair, speaking a
maiden's heart
Of fifteen summers, who would
fain depart
From ripening life's new-urgent
mystery,--
Love-choice of one too high her
love to be,--
But cannot yield her breath till
she has poured
Her strength away in this hot-
bleeding word,
Telling the secret of her soul to
her soul's lord."

Said Mico, "Nay, that thought is
poesy,
I need but listen as it sings to
me.
Come thou again to-morrow."
The third day,
When linked notes had
perfected the lay,
Minuccio had his summons to
the court,
To make, as he was wont, the
moments short
Of ceremonious dinner to the
king.
This was the time when he had
meant to bring
Melodious message of young
Lisa's love;
He waited till the air had ceased
to move
To ringing silver, till Falernian
wine

Made quickened sense with quietude combine;
And then with passionate descant made each ear incline.

Love, thou didst see me, light as morning's breath,
Roaming a garden in a joyous error,
Laughing at chases vain, a happy child,
Till of thy countenance the alluring terror
In majesty from out the blossoms smiled,
From out their life seeming a beauteous Death
O Love, who so didst choose me for thine own
Taking this little isle to thy great sway,
See now, it is the honour of thy

throne

That what thou gavest perish
not away,

Nor leave some sweet
remembrance to atone

By life that will be for the brief
life gone:

Hear, ere the shroud o'er these
frail limbs be thrown--

Since every king is vassal unto
thee,

My heart's lord needs must
listen loyally--

O tell him I am waiting for my
Death!

Tell him, for that he hath such
royal power

'Twere hard for him to think
how small a thing,

How slight a sign, would make a
wealthy dower

For one like me, the bride of

that pale king
Whose bed is mine at some
swift-nearing hour.
Go to my lord, and to his
memory bring
That happy birthday of my
sorrowing,
When his large glance made
meaner gazers glad,
Entering the bannered lists:
'twas then I had
The wound that laid me in the
arms of Death.
Tell him, O Love, I am a lowly
maid,
No more than any little knot of
thyme
That he with careless foot may
often tread;
Yet lowest fragrance oft will
mount sublime
And cleave to things most high
and hallowed,

As doth the fragrance of my
life's springtime,
My lowly love, that, soaring,
seeks to climb
Within his thought, and make a
gentle bliss,
More blissful than if mine, in
being his:
So shall I live in him, and rest in
Death.

The strain was new. It seemed a
pleading cry,
And yet a rounded, perfect
melody,
Making grief beauteous as the
tear-filled eyes
Of little child at little miseries.
Trembling at first, then swelling
as it rose,
Like rising light that broad and
broader grows,
It filled the hall, and so

possessed the air,
That not one living, breathing
soul was there,
Though dullest, slowest, but was
quivering
In Music's grasp, and forced to
hear her sing.
But most such sweet
compulsion took the mood
Of Pedro (tired of doing what he
would).
Whether the words which that
strange meaning bore
Were but the poet's feigning, or
aught more,
Was bounden question, since
their aim must be
At some imagined or true
royalty.
He called Minuccio, and bade
him tell
What poet of the day had writ
so well;

For, though they came behind
all former rhymes,
The verses were not bad for
these poor times.
"Monsignor, they are only three
days old,"
Minuccio said; "but it must not
be told
How this song grew, save to
your royal ear."
Eager, the king withdrew where
none was near,
And gave close audience to
Minuccio,
Who meetly told that love-tale
meet to know.
The king had features pliant to
confess
The presence of a manly
tenderness,--
Son, father, brother, lover, blent
in one,
In fine harmonic exaltation;

The spirit of religious chivalry.
He listened, and Minuccio could see
The tender, generous admiration spread
O'er all his face, and glorify his head
With royalty that would have kept its rank,
Though his brocaded robes to tatters shrank.
He answered without pause, "So sweet a maid,
In Nature's own insignia arrayed,
Though she were come of unmixed trading blood
That sold and bartered ever since the flood,
Would have the self-contained and single worth
Of radiant jewels born in darksome earth.

Raona were a shame to Sicily,
Letting such love and tears
unhonoured be:
Hasten, Minuccio, tell her that
the king
To-day will surely visit her when
vespers ring."

Joyful, Minuccio bore the joyous
word,
And told at full, while none but
Lisa heard,
How each thing had befallen,
sang the song,
And, like a patient nurse who
would prolong
All means of soothing, dwelt
upon each tone,
Each look, with which the
mighty Aragon
Marked the high worth his royal
heart assigned
To that dear place he held in

Lisa's mind.
She listened till the draughts of
pure content
Through all her limbs like some
new being went--
Life, not recovered, but untried
before,
From out the growing world's
unmeasured store
Of fuller, better, more divinely
mixed.
'Twas glad reverse: she had so
firmly fixed
To die, already seemed to fall a
veil
Shrouding the inner glow from
light of senses pale.

Her parents, wondering, see her
half arise;
Wondering, rejoicing, see her
long dark eyes
Brimful with clearness, not of

'scaping tears,
But of some light ethereal that
enspheres
Their orbs with calm, some
vision newly learnt
Where strangest fires erewhile
had blindly burnt.
She asked to have her soft white
robe and band
And coral ornaments; and with
her hand
She gave her long dark locks a
backward fall,
Then looked intently in a mirror
small,
And feared her face might,
perhaps, displease the king:
"In truth," she said, "I am a tiny
thing:
I was too bold to tell what could
such visit bring."

Meanwhile the king, revolving in

his thought
That innocent passion, was
more deeply wrought
To chivalrous pity; and at
vesper-bell,
With careless mien which hid his
purpose well,
Went forth on horseback, and,
as if by chance
Passing Bernardo's house, he
paused to glance
At the fine garden of this
wealthy man,
This Tuscan trader turned
Palermitan;
But, presently dismounting,
chose to walk
Amid the trellises, in gracious
talk
With this same trader, deigning
even to ask
If he had yet fulfilled the
father's task

Of marrying that daughter,
whose young charms
Himself, betwixt the passages of
arms,
Noted admiringly. "Monsignor,
no,
She is not married: that were
little woe,
Since she has counted barely
fifteen years;
But all such hopes of late have
turned to fears;
She droops and fades, though,
for a space quite brief,--
Scarce three hours past,--she
finds some strange relief."
The king avised: "'Twere dole to
all of us,
The world should lose a maid so
beauteous:
Let me now see her; since I am
her liege lord,
Her spirits must wage war with

death at my strong word."
In such half-serious playfulness,
he wends,
With Lisa's father and two
chosen friends,
Up to the chamber where she
pillowed sits,
Watching the door that opening
admits
A presence as much better than
her dreams,
As happiness than any longing
seems.
The king advanced, and, with a
reverent kiss
Upon her hand, said, "Lady,
what is this?
You, whose sweet youth should
others' solace be,
Pierce all our hearts, languishing
piteously.
We pray you, for the love of us,
be cheered,

Nor be too reckless of that life,
endeared
To us who know your passing
worthiness,
And count your blooming life as
part of our life's bliss."

Those words, that touch upon
her hand from him
Whom her soul worshipped, as
far seraphim
Worship the distant glory,
brought some shame
Quivering upon her cheek, yet
thrilled her frame
With such deep joy she seemed
in paradise,
In wondering gladness, and in
dumb surprise,
That bliss could be so blissful.
Then she spoke:
"Signor, I was too weak to bear
the yoke,

The golden yoke, of thoughts
too great for me;
That was the ground of my
infirmity.
But now I pray your grace to
have belief
That I shall soon be well, nor
any more cause grief."

The king alone perceived the
covert sense
Of all her words, which made
one evidence,
With her pure voice and candid
loveliness,
That he had lost much honour,
honouring less
That message of her passionate
distress.
He staid beside her for a little
while,
With gentle looks and speech,
until a smile

As placid as a ray of early morn
On opening flower-cups o'er her
lips was borne
When he had left her, and the
tidings spread
Through all the town, how he
had visited
The Tuscan trader's daughter,
who was sick,
Men said it was a royal deed,
and catholic.

And Lisa? She no longer wished
for death;
But as a poet, who sweet verses
saith
Within his soul, and joys in
music there,
Nor seeks another heaven, nor
can bear
Disturbing pleasures, so was she
content,
Breathing the life of grateful

sentiment.
She thought no maid betrothed
could be more blest;
For treasure must be valued by
the test
Of highest excellence and rarity,
And her dear joy was best as
best could be:
There seemed no other crown
to her delight,
Now the high loved one saw her
love aright.
Thus her soul thriving on that
exquisite mood,
Spread like the May-time all its
beauteous good
O'er the soft bloom of neck and
arms and cheek,
And strengthened the sweet
body, once so weak,
Until she rose and walked, and,
like a bird
With sweetly rippling throat,

she made her spring joys heard.

The king, when he the happy
change had seen,
Trusted the ear of Constance,
his fair queen,
With Lisa's innocent secret, and
conferred
How they should jointly, by their
deed and word,
Honour this maiden's love,
which, like the prayer
Of loyal hermits, never thought
to share
In what it gave. The queen had
that chief grace
Of womanhood, a heart that can
embrace
All goodness in another
woman's form;
And that same day, ere the sun
lay too warm
On southern terraces, a

messenger
Informed Bernardo that the
royal pair
Would straightway visit him,
and celebrate
Their gladness at his daughter's
happier state,
Which they were fain to see.
Soon came the king
On horseback, with his barons,
heralding
The advent of the queen in
courtly state;
And all, descending at the
garden gate,
Streamed with their feathers,
velvet, and brocade,
Through the pleached alleys, till
they, pausing, made
A lake of splendour 'mid the
aloes grey;
When, meekly facing all their
proud array,

The white-robed Lisa with her
parents stood,
As some white dove before the
gorgeous brood
Of dapple-breasted birds born
by the Colchian flood.
The king and queen, by gracious
looks and speech,
Encourage her, and thus their
courtiers teach
How, this fair morning, they
may courtliest be,
By making Lisa pass it happily.
And soon the ladies and the
barons all
Draw her by turns, as at a
festival
Made for her sake, to easy, gay
discourse,
And compliment with looks and
smiles enforce;
A joyous hum is heard the
gardens round;

Soon there is Spanish dancing,
and the sound
Of minstrel's song, and autumn
fruits are pluckt;
Till mindfully the king and queen
conduct
Lisa apart to where a trellised
shade
Made pleasant resting. Then
King Pedro said,--
"Excellent maiden, that rich gift
of love
Your heart hath made us hath a
worth above
All royal treasures, nor is fitly
met
Save when the grateful memory
of deep debt
Lies still behind the outward
honours done:
And as a sign that no oblivion
Shall overflood that faithful
memory,

We while we live your cavalier
will be;
Nor will we ever arm ourselves
for fight,
Whether for struggle dire, or
brief delight
Of warlike feigning, but we first
will take
The colours you ordain, and for
your sake
Charge the more bravely where
your emblem is:
Nor will we claim from you an
added bliss
To our sweet thoughts of you
save one sole kiss.
But there still rests the outward
honour meet
To mark your worthiness; and
we entreat
That you will turn your ear to
proffered vows
Of one who loves you, and

would be your spouse
We must not wrong yourself
and Sicily
By letting all your blooming
years pass by
Unmated: you will give the
world its due
From beauteous maiden, and
become a matron true."

Then Lisa, wrapt in virgin
wonderment
At her ambitious love's
complete content,
Which left no further good for
her to seek
Than love's obedience, said,
with accent meek,--
"Monsignor, I know well that
were it known
To all the world how high my
love had flown,
There would be few who would

not deem me mad,
Or say my mind the falsest
image had
Of my condition and your
loftiness.
But Heaven has seen that for no
moment's space
Have I forgotten you to be the
king,
Or me myself to be a lowly
thing--
A little lark, enamoured of the
sky,
That soared to sing, to break its
breast, and die.
But, as you better know than I,
the heart
In choosing chooseth not its
own desert,
But that great merit which
attracteth it:
'Tis law, I struggled, but I must
submit,

And having seen a worth all
worth above,
I loved you, love you, and shall
always love.
But that doth mean, my will is
ever yours,
Not only when your will my
good insures,
But if it wrought me what the
world calls harm:
Fire, wounds, would wear from
your dear will a charm.
That you will be my knight is full
content,
And for that kiss,--I pray, first,
for the queen's consent."
Her answer, given with such
firm gentleness,
Pleased the queen well, and
made her hold no less
Of Lisa's merit than the king had
held.
And so, all cloudy threats of

grief dispelled,
There was betrothal made that
very morn
'Twixt Perdicone, youthful,
brave, well-born,
And Lisa whom he loved; she
loving well
The lot that from obedience
befell.
The queen a rare betrothal ring
on each
Bestowed, and other gems, with
gracious speech.
And, that no joy might lack, the
king, who knew
The youth was poor, gave him
rich Ceffalu
And Cataletta,--large and fruitful
lands,--
Adding much promise when he
joined their hands.
At last he said to Lisa, with an
air

Gallant yet noble, "Now we
claim our share
From your sweet love, a share
which is not small;
For in the sacrament one crumb
is all."
Then, taking her small face his
hands between,
He kissed her on the brow with
kiss serene,--
Fit seal to that pure vision her
young soul had seen.

And many witnessed that King
Pedro kept
His royal promise. Perdicone
stept
To many honours honourably
won,
Living with Lisa in true union.
Throughout his life, the king still
took delight
To call himself fair Lisa's faithful

knight;
And never wore in field or
tournament
A scarf or emblem, save by Lisa
sent.
Such deeds made subjects loyal
in that land;
They joyed that one so worthy
to command,
So chivalrous and gentle, had
become
The king of Sicily, and filled the
room
Of Frenchmen, who abused the
Church's trust,
Till, in a righteous vengeance on
their lust,
Messina rose, with God, and
with the dagger's thrust.

L'ENVOI.

Reader, this story pleased me
long ago
In the bright pages of Boccaccio;
And where the author of a good
we know,
Let us not fail to pay the grateful
thanks we owe.

The Legend Of Jubal

When Cain was driven from
Jehovah's land
He wandered eastward, seeking
some far strand
Ruled by kind gods who asked
no offerings
Save pure field-fruits, as
aromatic things,
To feed the subtler sense of
frames divine
That lived on fragrance for their
food and wine:
Wild joyous gods, who winked
at faults and folly,
And could be pitiful and
melancholy.
He never had a doubt that such
gods were;
He looked within, and saw them
mirrored there.

Some think he came at last to
Tartary,
And some to Ind; but,
howsoe'er it be,
His staff he planted where
sweet waters ran,
And in that home of Cain the
Arts began.
Man's life was spacious in the
early world:
It paused, like some slow ship
with sail unfurled
Waiting in seas by scarce a
wavelet curled;
Beheld the slow star-paces of
the skies,
And grew from strength to
strength through centuries;
Saw infant trees fill out their
giant limbs,
And heard a thousand
times the sweet birds' marriage
hymns.

In Cain's young city none had
heard of Death
Save him, the founder; and it
was his faith
That here, away from harsh
Jehovah's law,
Man was immortal, since no halt
or flaw
In Cain's own frame betrayed six
hundred years,
But dark as pines that autumn
never sears
His locks thronged backward as
he ran, his frame
Rose like the orbed sun each
morn the same,
Lake-mirrored to his gaze; and
that red brand,
The scorching impress of
Jehovah's hand,
Was still clear-edged to his
unwearied eye,

Its secret firm in time-fraught
memory.
He said, "My happy offspring
shall not know
That the red life from out a man
may flow
When smitten by his brother."
True, his race
Bore each one stamped upon
his new-born face
A copy of the brand no whit less
clear;
But every mother held that little
copy dear.
Thus generations in glad idlesse
throve,
Nor hunted prey, nor with each
other strove;
For clearest springs were
plenteous in the land,
And gourds for cups; the ripe
fruits sought the hand,

Bending the laden boughs with
fragrant gold;
And for their roofs and
garments wealth untold
Lay everywhere in grasses and
broad leaves:
They laboured gently, as a maid
who weaves
Her hair in mimic mats, and
pauses oft
And strokes across her hand the
tresses soft,
Then peeps to watch the poised
butterfly,
Or little burthened ants that
homeward hie.
Time was but leisure to their
lingering thought,
There was no' need for haste to
finish aught;
But sweet beginnings were
repeated still

Like infant babblings that no
task fulfil;
For love, that loved not change,
constrained the simple will.
Till, hurling stones in mere
athletic joy,
Strong Lamech struck and killed
his fairest boy,
And tried to wake him with the
tenderest cries,
And fetched and held before the
glazed eyes
The things they best had loved
to look upon;
But never glance or smile or sigh
he won.
The generations stood around
those twain
Helplessly gazing, till their father
Cain
Parted the press, and said, " He
will not wake;

This is the endless sleep, and we
must make
A bed deep down for him
beneath the sod;
For know, my sons, there is a
mighty God
Angry with all man's race, but
most with me.
I fled from out His land in vain!
—'tis He
Who came and slew the lad; for
He has found
This home of ours, and we shall
all be bound
By the harsh bands of His most
cruel will,
Which any moment may some
dear one kill.
Nay, though we live for
countless moons, at last
We and all ours shall die like
summers past.

This is Jehovah's will, and He is
strong;
I thought the way I travelled
was too long
For Him to follow me: my
thought was vain!
He walks unseen, but leaves a
track of pain,
Pale Death His footprint is, and
He will come again!"
And a new spirit from that hour
came o'er
The race of Cain: soft idlesse
was no more,
But even the sunshine had a
heart of care,
Smiling with hidden dread- a
mother fair
Who folding to her breast a
dying child
Beams with feigned joy that but
makes sadness mild.

Death was now lord of Life, and
at his word
Time, vague as air before, new
terrors stirred,
With measured wing now
audibly arose
Throbbing through all things to
some unknown close.
Now glad Content by clutching
Haste was torn,
And Work grew eager, and
Device was born.
It seemed the light was never
loved before,
Now each man said, "Twill go
and come no more."
No budding branch, no pebble
from the brook,
No form, no shadow, but new
dearness took
From the one thought that life
must have an end;

And the last parting now began
to send
Diffusive dread through love
and wedded bliss,
Thrilling them into finer
tenderness.
Then Memory disclosed her face
divine,
That like the calm nocturnal
lights doth shine
Within the soul, and shows the
sacred graves,
And shows the presence that no
sunlight craves,
No space, no warmth, but
moves among them all;
Gone and yet here, and
coming at each call,
With ready voice and eyes that
understand,
And lips that ask a kiss, and dear
responsive hand.

Thus to Cain's race death was
tear-watered seed
Of various life and action-
shaping need.
But chief 'the sons of Lamech
felt the stings
Of new ambition, and the force
that springs
In passion beating on the shores
of fate.
They said, " There comes a night
when all too late
The mind shall long to prompt
the achieving hand,
The eager thought behind
closed portals stand,
And the last wishes to the mute
lips press
Buried ere death in silent
helplessness.
Then while the soul its way with
sound can cleave,

And while the arm is strong to
strike and heave,
Let soul and arm give shape that
will abide
And rule above our graves, and
power divide
With that great god of day,
whose rays must bend
As we shall make the moving
shadows tend.
Come, let us. fashion acts that
are to be,
When we shall lie in darkness
silently,
As our young brother doth,
whom yet we see
Fallen and slain, but reigning in
our will
By that one image of him pale
and still."
For Lamech's sons were heroes
of their race:

Jabal, the eldest, bore upon his
face
The look of that calm river-god,
the Nile,
Mildly secure in power that
needs not guile.
But Tubal-Cain was restless as
the fire
That glows and spreads and
leaps from high to higher
Where'er is aught to seize or to
subdue;
Strong as a storm he lifted or
o'erthrew,
His urgent limbs like rounded
granite grew,
Such granite as the plunging
torrent wears
And roaring rolls around
through countless years.
But strength that still on
movement must be fed,

Inspiring thought of change,
devices bred,
And urged his mind through
earth and air to rove
For force that he could conquer
if he strove,
For lurking forms that might
new tasks fulfil
And yield unwilling to his
stronger-will.
Such Tubal-Cain. But Jubal had a
frame
Fashioned to finer senses, which
became
A yearning for some
hidden soul of things,
Some outward touch complete
on inner springs
That vaguely moving bred a
lonely pain,
A want that did but stronger
grow with gain

Of all good else, as spirits might
be sad
For lack of speech to tell us they
are glad.
Now Jabal learned to tame the
lowing kine,
And from their udders drew the
snow-white wine
That stirs the innocent joy, and
makes the stream
Of elemental life with fulness
teem;
The star-browed calves he
nursed With feeding hand,
And sheltered them, till all the
little band
Stood mustered gazing at the
sunset way
Whence he would come with
store at close of day.
He soothed the silly sheep with
friendly tone,

And reared their staggering
lambs, that, older grown,
Followed his steps with sense-
taught memory;
Till he, their shepherd, could
their leader be,
And guide them through the
pastures as he would,
With sway that grew from
ministry of good.
He spread his tents upon the
grassy plain
Which, eastward widening like
the open main,
Showed the first whiteness
'neath the morning star;
Near him his sister, deft, as
women are,
Plied her quick skill in sequence
to his thought
Till the hid treasures of the milk
she caught

Revealed like pollen 'mid the
petals white,
The golden pollen, virgin to the
light.
Even the she-wolf with young,
on rapine bent,
He caught and tethered in his
mat-walled tent,
And cherished all her little
sharp-nosed young
Till the small race with hope and
terror clung
About his footsteps, till each
new-reared brood,
Remoter from the memories of
the wood,
More glad discerned their
common home with man.
This was the work of Jabal: he
began
The pastoral life, and, sire of
joys to be,

Spread the sweet ties that bind
the family
O'er dear dumb souls that
thrilled at man's caress,
And shared his pain with patient
helpfulness.
But Tubal-Cain had caught and
yoked the fire,
Yoked it with stones that bent
the flaming spire
And made it roar in prisoned
servitude
Within the furnace, till with
force subdued
It changed all forms he willed to
work upon,
Till hard from soft,-and soft
from hard, he won.
The pliant clay he moulded as
he would,
And laughed with joy when 'mid
the heat it stood

Shaped as his hand had chosen,
while the mass
That from his hold, dark,
obstinate, would pass,
He drew all glowing from the
busy heat,
All breathing as with life that he
could beat
With thundering hammer,
making it obey
His will creative, like the pale
soft clay.
Each day he wrought and better
than he planned,
Shape breeding shape beneath
his restless hand.
(The soul without still helps the
soul within,
And its deft magic ends what we
begin.)
Nay, in his dreams his hammer
he would wield

And seem to see a myriad types
revealed,
Then spring with wondering
triumphant cry,
And, lest the inspiring vision
should go by,
Would rush to labour with that
plastic zeal
Which all the passion of our life
can steal
For force to work with. Each day
saw the birth
Of various forms, which, flung
upon the earth,
Seemed harmless toys to cheat
the exacting hour,
But were as seeds instinct with
hidden power.
The axe, the club, the spiked
wheel, the chain,
Held silently the shrieks and
moans of pain;

And near them latent lay in
share and spade,
In the strong bar, the saw, and
deep-curved blade,
Glad voices of the hearth and
harvest-home,
The social good, and all earth's
joy to come.
Thus to mixed ends wrought
Tubal; and they say,
Some things he made have
lasted to this day;
As, thirty silver pieces that were
found
By Noah's children
buried in the ground.
He made them from mere
hunger of device,
Those small white' discs; but
they became the price
The traitor Judas sold his Master
for;

And men still handling them in
peace and war
Catch foul disease, that comes
as appetite,
And lurks and clings as
withering, damning blight.
But Tubal-Cain wot not of
treachery,
Nor greedy lust, nor any ill to
be,
Save the one ill of sinking into
nought,
Banished from action and act-
shaping thought.
He was the sire of swift-
transforming skill,
Which arms for conquest man's
ambitious will;
And round him gladly, as his
hammer rung,
Gathered the elders and the
growing young:

These handled vaguely, and
those plied the tools,
Till, happy chance begetting
conscious rules,
The home of Cain with industry
was rife,
And glimpses of a strong
persistent life,
Panting through generations as
one breath,
And filling with its soul the blank
of death.
Jubal, too, watched the
hammer, till his eyes,
No longer following its fall or
rise,
Seemed glad with something
that they could not see,
But only listened to - some
melody,
Wherein dumb longings inward
speech had found,

Won from the common store of
struggling sound.
Then, as the metal shapes more
various grew,
And, hurled upon each other,
resonance drew,
Each gave new tones, the
revelations dim
Of some external soul that
spoke for him:
The hollow vessel's clang, the
clash, the boom,
Like light that makes wide
spiritual room
And skyey spaces in the
spaceless thought,
To Jubal such enlarged passion
brought,
That love, hope, rage, and all
experience,
Were fused in vaster being,
fetching thence

Concords and discords,
cadences and cries
That seemed from some world-
shrouded soul to rise,
Some rapture more intense,
some mightier rage,
Some living sea that burst the
bounds of man's brief age.
Then with such blissful trouble
and glad care
For growth. within unborn as
mothers bear,
To the far woods he wandered,
listening,
And heard the birds their little
stories sing
In notes whose rise and fall
seem melted speech—
Melted with tears, smiles,
glances —that can reach
More quickly through our
frame's deep-winding night,

And without thought raise
thought's best fruit, delight.
Pondering, he sought his home
again and heard
The fluctuant changes of the
spoken word:
The deep remonstrance and the
argued want,
Insistent first in close
monotonous chant,
Next leaping upward to defiant
stand
Or downward beating like the
resolute hand;
The mother's call, the children's
answering cry,
The laugh's light cataract
tumbling from on high;
The suasive repetitions Jabal
taught,
That timid browsing cattle
homeward brought:

The clear-winged fugue of
echoes vanishing;
And through them all the
hammer's rhythmic ring.
Jubal sat lonely, all around was
dim,
Yet his face glowed with light
revealed to him:
For as the delicate stream of
odour wakes
The thought-wed sentience, and
some image makes
From out the mingled fragments
of the past,
Finely compact in wholeness
that will last,
So streamed as from the body
of each sound
Subtler pulsations, swift as
warmth, which found
All prisoned germs and all their
powers unbound,

Till thought self-luminous
flamed from memory,
And in creative vision wandered
free.
Then Jubal, standing, rapturous
arms upraised,
And on the dark with eager eyes
he gazed,
As had some manifested god
been there.
It was his thought he saw: the
presence fair
Of unachieved achievement, the
high task,
The mighty unborn spirit that
doth ask
With irresistible cry for blood
and breath,
Till feeding its great life we sink
in death.
He said, "Were now those
mighty tones and cries

That from the giant soul of earth
arise,
Those groans of some great
travail heard from far,
Some power at wrestle with the
things that are,
Those sounds which vary with
the varying form
Of clay and metal, and in
sightless swarm
Fill the wide space with tremors:
were these wed
To human voices with such
passion fed
As does but glimmer in our
common speech,
But might flame out in tones
whose changing reach
Surpassing meagre need,
informs the sense
With fuller union, finer
difference—

Were this great vision, now
obscurely bright
As morning hills that melt in
new-poured light,
Wrought into solid form and
living sound,
Moving with ordered throb and
sure rebound,
Then——Nay, I Jubal will that
work begin!
The generations of our race
shall win
New life, that grows from out
the heart of this,
As spring from winter, or as
lovers' bliss
From out the dull unknown of
unwaked energies."
Thus he resolved, and in the
soul-fed light
Of coming ages waited through
the night,

Watching for that near dawn
whose chiller ray
Showed but the unchanged
world of yesterday;
Where all the order of his
dream divine
Lay like Olympian forms within
the mine;
Where fervour that could fill the
earthly round
With thronged joys of form-
begotten sound
Must shrink intense within the
patient power
That lonely labours through the
niggard hour.
Such patience have the heroes
who begin,
Sailing the first toward lands
which others win.
Jubal must dare as great
beginners dare,

Strike form's first way in matter
rude and bare,
And, yearning vaguely toward
the plenteous choir
Of the world's harvest, make
one poor small lyre.
He made it, and from out its
measured frame
Drew the harmonic soul, whose
answers came
With guidance sweet and
lessons of delight
Teaching to ear and hand the
blissful Right,
Where strictest law is gladness
to-the sense,
And all desire bends toward
obedience.
Then Jubal poured his triumph
in a song—
The rapturous word that
rapturous notes prolong

As radiance streams from
smallest things that burn,
Or thought of loving into love
doth turn.
And still his lyre gave
companionship
In sense-taught concert as of lip
with lip.
Alone amid the hills at first he
tried
His winged song; then with
adoring pride
And bridegroom's joy at leading
forth his bride,
He said, "This wonder which my
soul hath found,
This heart of music in the might
of sound,
Shall forthwith be the share of
all our race,
And like the morning gladden
common space:

The song shall spread and swell
as rivers do,
And I will teach our youth with
skill to woo
This living lyre, to know its
secret will;
Its fine division of the good and
ill..
So shall men call me sire of
harmony,
And where great Song is, there
my life shall be."
Thus glorying as a god
beneficent,
Forth from his solitary joy he
went
To bless mankind. It was at
evening,
When shadows lengthen from
each westward thing,
When imminence of change
makes sense more fine,

And light seems holier in its
grand decline.
The fruit-trees wore their
studded coronal,
Earth and her children were at
festival,
Glowing as with one heart and
one consent—
Thought, love, trees, rocks, in
sweet warm radiance blent.
The tribe of Cain was resting on
the ground,
The various ages wreathed in
one broad round.
Here lay, while children peeped
o'er his huge thighs,
The sinewy man embrowned by
centuries;
Here the broad-bosomed
mother of the strong
Looked, like Demeter, placid
o'er the throng

Of young lithe forms whose rest
was movement too—
Tricks, prattle, nods, and laughs
that lightly flew,
And swayings as of flower-beds
where Love blew.
For all had feasted well upon
the flesh
Of juicy fruits, on nuts, and
honey fresh,
And now their wine was health-
bred merriment,
Which through the generations
circling went,
Leaving none sad, for even
father Cain
Smiled as a Titan might,
despising pain.
Jabal sat circled with a playful
ring
Of children, lambs and whelps,
whose gambolling,

With tiny hoofs, paws, hands,
and dimpled feet,
Made barks, bleats, laughs, in
pretty hubbub meet.
But Tubal's hammer rang from
far away,
Tubal alone would keep no
holiday,
His furnace must not slack for
any feast,
For of all hardship, work he
counted least;
He scorned all rest but sleep,
where every dream
Made his repose more potent
action seem.
Yet with health's nectar some
strange thirst was blent,
The fateful growth, the
unnamed discontent,
The inward shaping toward
some unborn power,

Some deeper-breathing act, the
being's flower.
After all gestures, words, and
speech of eyes,
The soul had more to tell, and
broke in sighs.
Then from the east, with glory
on his head
Such as low-slanting beams on
corn-waves spread,
Came Jubal with his lyre: there
'mid the throng,
Where the blank space was,
poured a solemn song,
Touching his lyre to full
harmonic throb
And measured pulse, with
cadences that sob,
Exult and cry, and search the
inmost deep
Where the dark sources of new
passion sleep.

Joy took the air, and took each
breathing soul,
Embracing them in one
entranced whole,
Yet thrilled each varying frame
to various ends,
As Spring new-waking through
the creature sends
Or rage or tenderness; more
plenteous life
Here breeding dread, and there
a fiercer strife.
He who had lived through twice
three centuries,
Whose months monotonous,
like trees on trees
In hoary forests, stretched a
backward maze,
Dreamed himself dimly through
the travelled days
Till in clear light he paused, and
felt the sun

That warmed him when he was
a little one;
Knew that true heaven, the
recovered past,
The dear small Known amid the
Unknown vast,
And in that heaven wept. But
younger limbs
Thrilled toward the future, that
bright land which swims
In western glory, isles and
streams and bays,
Where hidden pleasures float in
golden haze.
And in all these the rhythmic
influence,
Sweetly o'ercharging the
delighted sense,
Flowed out in movements, little
waves that spread
Enlarging, till in tidal union led
The youths and maidens both
alike long-tressed,

By grace-inspiring melody
possessed,
Rose in slow dance, with
beauteous floating swerve
Of limbs and hair, and many a
melting curve
Of ringed feet swayed by each
close-linked palm:
Then Jubal poured, more
rapture in his psalm,
The dance fired music, music
fired the dance,
The glow diffusive lit each
countenance,
Till all the circling tribe arose
and stood
With glad yet awful shock of
that mysterious good.
Even Tubal caught the sound,
and wondering came,
Urging his sooty bulk like
smoke-wrapt flame

Till he could see his brother with
the lyre,
The work for which he lent his
furnace-fire
And diligent hammer, witting
nought of this
This power in metal shape
which made strange bliss,
Entering within him like a dream
full-fraught
With new creations finished in a
thought.
The sun had sunk, but music still
was there,
And when this ceased, still
triumph filled the air:
It seemed the stars were shining
with delight
And that no night was ever like
this night.
All clung with praise to Jubal:
some besought

That he would teach them his
new skill; some caught,
Swiftly as smiles are caught in
looks that meet,
The tone's melodic change and
rhythmic beat:
'Twas easy following where
invention trod—
All eyes can see when light flows
out from God.
And thus did Jubal to his race
reveal
Music their larger soul, where
woe and weal
Filling the resonant chords, the
song, the dance,
Moved with a wider-winged
utterance.
Now many a lyre was fashioned,
many a song
Raised echoes new, old echoes
to prolong,

Till things of Jubal's making
were so rife,
"Hearing myself," he said, "I
hems in my life,
And I will get me to some far-off
land,
Where higher mountains under
heaven stand
And touch the blue at rising of
the stars,
Whose song they hear where no
rough mingling mars
The great clear voices. Such
lands there must be,
Where varying forms make
varying symphony
Where other thunders roll amid
the hills,
Some mightier wind a mightier
forest fills
With other strains through
other-shapen boughs;

Where bees and birds and
beasts that hunt or browse
Will teach me songs I know not.
Listening there,
My life shall grow like trees both
tall and fair
That rise and spread and bloom
toward fuller fruit each year."
He took a raft, and travelled
with the stream
Southward for many a league,
till he might deem
He saw at last the pillars of the
sky,
Beholding mountains whose
white majesty
Rushed through him as new
awe, and made new song
That swept with fuller wave the
chords along,
Weighting his voice with deep
religious chime,.

The iteration of slow chant
sublime.
It was the region long inhabited
By all the race of Seth; and Jubal
said,
"Here have I found my thirsty
soul's desire,
Eastward the hills touch heaven,
and evening's fire
Flames through deep waters, I
will take my rest,
And feed anew from my great
mother's breast,
The sky-clasped Earth, whose
voices nurture me
As the flowers' sweetness doth
the honey-bee."
He lingered wandering for many
an age,
And, sowing music, made high
heritage
For generations far beyond the
Flood

For the poor late-begotten
human brood
Born to life's weary brevity and
perilous good.
And ever as he travelled he
would climb
The farthest mountain, yet the
heavenly chime,
The mighty tolling of the far-off
spheres
Beating their pathway, never
touched his ears.
But wheresoe'er he rose, the
heavens rose,
And the far-gazing mountain
could disclose
Nought but a wider earth; until
one height
Showed him the ocean
stretched in liquid light,
And he could hear its
multitudinous roar,

Its plunge and hiss upon the
pebbled shore:
Then Jubal silent sat, and
touched his lyre no more.
He thought, "The world is great,
but I am weak,
And where the sky bends is no
solid peak
To give me footing, but instead,
this main
Like myriad maddened horses
thundering o'er the plain.
"New voices come to me
where'er I roam,
My heart too widens with its
widening home:
But song grows weaker, and the
heart must break
For lack of voice, or fingers that
can wake
The lyre's full answer; nay, its
chords were all

Too few to meet the growing spirit's call.
The former songs seem little, yet no more
Can soul, hand, voice, with interchanging lore
Tell what the earth is saying unto me:
The secret is too great, I hear confusedly.
"No farther will I travel: once again
My brethren I will see, and that fair plain
Where I and song were born.
There fresh-voiced youth
Will pour my strains with all the early truth
Which now abides not in my voice and hands,
But only in the soul, the will that stands

Helpless to move. My tribe
remembering Will cry,
' 'Tis he!' and run to greet me,
welcoming."
The way was weary. Many a
date-palm grew,
And shook out clustered gold
against the blue,
While Jubal, guided by the
steadfast spheres,
Sought the dear home of those
first eager years,
When, with fresh vision fed, the
fuller will
Took living outward shape in
pliant skill;
For still he hoped to find the
former things,
And the warm gladness
recognition brings.
His footsteps erred among the
mazy woods

And long illusive sameness of
the floods,
Winding and wandering.
Through far regions, strange
With Gentile homes and faces,
did he range,
And left his music in their
memory,
And left at last, when nought
besides would free
His homeward steps from
clinging hands and cries,
The ancient lyre. And now in
ignorant eyes
No sign remained of Jubal,
Lamech's son,
That mortal frame wherein was
first begun
The immortal life of song. His
withered brow
Pressed over eyes that held no
lightning now,

His locks streamed whiteness on
the hurrying air,
The unresting soul had worn
itself quite bare
Of beauteous token, as the
outworn might
Of oaks slow dying, gaunt in
summer's light.
His full deep voice toward
thinnest treble ran:
He was the rune-writ story of a
man.
And so at last he neared the
well-known land,
Could see the hills in ancient
order stand
With friendly faces whose
familiar gaze
Looked through the sunshine of
his childish days;
Knew the deep-shadowed folds
of hanging woods,

And seemed to see the selfsame
insect broods
Whirling and quivering o'er the
flowers —to hear
The selfsame cuckoo making
distance near.
Yea, the dear Earth, with
mother's constancy,
Met and embraced him, and
said, "Thou art he!
This was thy cradle, here my
breast was thine,
Where feeding, thou didst all
thy life intwine
With my skly-wedded life in
heritage divine."
But wending ever through the
watered plain,
Firm not to rest save in the
home of Cain,
He saw dread Change, with
dubious face and cold

That never kept a welcome for
the old,
Like some strange heir upon the
hearth, arise
Saying, "This home is mine." He
thought his eyes
Mocked all deep memories, as
things new made,
Usurping sense, make old things
shrink and fade
And seem ashamed to meet the
staring day.
His memory saw a small foot-
trodden way,
His eyes a broad far-stretching
paven road
Bordered with many a tomb and
fair abode;
The little city that once nestled
low
As buzzing groups about some
central glow,

Spread like a murmuring crowd
o'er plain and steep,
Or monster huge in heavy-
breathing sleep.
His heart grew faint, and
tremblingly he sank
Close by the wayside on a weed-
grown bank,
Not far from where a new-
raised temple stood,
Sky-roofed, and fragrant with
wrought cedar-wood.
The morning sun was high; his
rays fell hot
On this hap-chosen, dusty,
common spot,
On the dry withered grass and
withered man:
That wondrous frame where
melody began
Lay as a tomb defaced that no
eye cared to scan.

But while he sank far music
reached his ear.
He listened until wonder
silenced fear,
And gladness wonder; for the
broadening stream
Of sound advancing was his
early dream,
Brought like fulfilment of
forgotten prayer;
As if his soul, breathed out upon
the air,
Had held the invisible seeds of
harmony
Quick with the various strains of
life to be.
He listened: the sweet mingled
difference
With charm alternate took the
meeting sense;
Then bursting like some shield-
broad lily red,

Sudden and near the trumpet's notes out-spread,
And soon his eyes could see the metal flower,
Shining upturned, out on the morning pour
Its incense audible; could see a train
From out the street slow-winding on the plain
With lyres and cymbals, flutes and psalteries,
While men, youths, maids, in concert sang to these
With various throat, or in succession poured,
Or in full volume mingled. But one word
Ruled each recurrent rise and answering fall,
As when the multitudes adoring call

On some great name divine,
their common soul,
The common need, love, joy,
that knits them in one whole.
The word was "Jubal!".. "Jubal"
filled the air,
And seemed to ride aloft, a
spirit there,
Creator of the choir, the full-
fraught strain
That grateful rolled itself to him
again.
The aged man adust upon the
bank—
Whom no eye saw— at first
with rapture drank
The bliss of music, then, with
swelling heart,
Felt, this was his own being's
greater part,
The universal joy once born in
him.

But when the train, with living
face and limb
And vocal breath, came nearer
and more near,
The longing grew that they
should hold him dear;
Him, Lamech's son, whom all
their fathers knew,
The breathing Jubal —him, to
whom their love was due.
All was forgotten but the
burning need
To claim his fuller self, to claim
the deed
That lived away from him, and
grew apart,
While he as from a tomb, with
lonely heart,
Warmed by no meeting glance,
no hand that pressed,
Lay chill amid the life his life had
blessed.

What though his song should
spread from man's small race
Out through the myriad worlds
that people space,
And make the heavens one joy-
diffusing quire?
Still 'mid that vast would throb
the keen desire
Of this poor aged flesh, this
eventide,
This twilight soon in darkness to
subside,
This little pulse of self, that,
having glowed
Through thrice three centuries,
and divinely strewed
The light of music through the
vague of sound,
Ached smallness still in good
that had no bound.
For no eye saw him, while with
loving pride—

Each voice with each in praise of
Jubal vied.
Must he in conscious trance,
dumb, helpless lie
While all that ardent kindred
passed him by?
His flesh cried out to live with
living men,
And join that soul which to the
inward ken
Of all the hymning train was
present there.
Strong passion's daring sees not
aught to dare:
The frost-locked starkness of his
frame low-bent,
His voice's penury of tones long
spent,
He felt not; all his being leaped
in flame
To meet his kindred as they
onward came

Slackening and wheeling toward
the temple's face:
He rushed before them to the
glittering space,
And, with a strength that was
but strong desire,
Cried, "I am Jubal, I! . . . I made
the lyre!"
The tones amid a lake of silence
fell
Broken and strained, as if a
feeble bell
Had tuneless pealed the
triumph of a land
To listening crowds in
expectation spanned.
Sudden came showers of
laughter on that lake;
They spread along the train
from front to wake
In one great storm of
merriment, while he

Shrank doubting whether he
could Jubal be,
And not a dream of Jubal,
whose rich vein
Of passionate music came with
that dream-pain,
Wherein the sense slips off from
each loved thing,
And all appearance is mere
vanishing.
But ere the laughter died from
out the rear,
Anger in front saw profanation
near;
Jubal was but a name in each
man's faith
For glorious power untouched
by that slow death
Which creeps with creeping
time; this too, the spot,
And this the day, it must be
crime to blot,

Even with scoffing at a
madman's lie:
Jubal was not a name to wed
with mockery.
Two rushed upon him: two, the
most devout
In honour of great Jubal, thrust
him out,
And beat him with their flutes.
'Twas little need;
He strove not, cried not, but
with tottering speed,
As if the scorn and howls were
driving wind
That urged his body, serving so
the mind
Which could but shrink and
yearn, he sought the screen
Of thorny thickets, and there fell
unseen.
The immortal name of Jubal
filled the sky,

While Jubal lonely laid him
down to die.
He said within his soul, "This is
the end:
O'er all the earth to where the
heavens bend
And hem men's travel, I have
breathed my soul:
I lie here now the remnant of
that whole,
The embers of a life, a lonely
pain;
As far-off rivers to my thirst
were vain,
So of my mighty years nought
comes to me again.
"Is the day sinking? Softest
coolness springs
From something round me:
dewy shadowy wings
Enclose me all around — no, not
above—

Is moonlight there? I see a face
of love,
Fair as sweet music when my
heart was strong:
Yea— art thou come again to
me, great Song?"
The face bent over him like
silver night
In long-remembered summers;
that calm light
Of days which shine in
firmaments of thought,
That past unchangeable, from
change still wrought.
And there were tones that with
the vision blent:
He knew not if that gaze the
music sent,
Or music that calm gaze: to
hear, to see,
Was but one undivided ecstasy:
The raptured senses melted into
one,

And parting life a moment's
freedom won
From in and outer, as a little
child
Sits on a bank and sees blue
heavens mild
Down in the water, and
forgets its limbs,
And knoweth nought save the
blue heaven that swims.
"Jubal," the face said, " I am thy
loved Past,
The soul that makes thee one
from first to last.
I am the angel of thy life and
death,
Thy outbreathed being drawing
its last breath.
Am I not thine alone, a dear
dead bride
Who blest thy lot above all
men's beside?

Thy bride whom thou wouldst
never change, nor take
Any bride living, for that dead
one's sake?
Was I not all thy yearning and
delight,
Thy chosen search, thy senses'
beauteous Right,
Which still had been the hunger
of thy frame
In central heaven, hadst thou
been still the same?
Wouldst thou have asked aught
else from any god
Whether with gleaming feet on
earth he trod
Or thundered through the skies
— aught else for share
Of mortal good, than in thy soul
to bear
The growth of song, and feel the
sweet unrest

Of the world's spring-tide in thy
conscious breast?
No, thou hadst grasped thy lot
with all its pain,
Nor loosed it any painless lot to
gain
Where music's voice was silent;
for thy fate
Was human music's self
incorporate:
Thy senses' keenness and thy
passionate strife
Were flesh of her flesh and her
womb of life.
And greatly hast thou lived, for
not alone
With hidden raptures were her
secrets shown,
Buried within thee, as the
purple light
Of gems may sleep in solitary
night;

But thy expanding joy was still
to give,
And with the generous air in
song to live
Feeding the wave of ever-
widening bliss
Where fellowship means equal
perfectness.
And on the mountains in thy
wandering
Thy feet were beautiful as
blossomed spring,
That turns the leafless wood to
love's glad home,
For with thy coming Melody was
come.
This was thy lot, to feel, create,
bestow,
And that immeasurable life to
know
From which the fleshly self falls
shrivelled, dead,

A seed primeval that has forests
bred.
It is the glory of the heritage
Thy life has left, that makes thy
outcast age:
Thy limbs shall lie dark,
tombless on this sod,
Because thou shinest in man's
soul, a god,
Who found and gave new
passion and new joy
That nought but Earth's
destruction can destroy.
Thy gifts to give was thine of
men alone:
'Twas but in giving that thou
couldst atone
For too much wealth amid their
poverty."—
The words seemed melting into
symphony,
The wings upbore him, and the
gazing song

Was floating him the heavenly
space along,
Where mighty harmonies all
gently fell
Through veiling vastness, like
the far-off bell,
Till, ever onward through the
choral blue,
He heard more faintly and more
faintly knew,
Quitting mortality, a quenched
sun-wave,
The All-creating Presence for his
grave.

A Minor Prophet

I have a friend, a vegetarian
seer,
By name Elias Baptist
Butterworth,
A harmless, bland, disinterested
man,
Whose ancestors in Cromwell's
day believed
The Second Advent certain in
five years,
But when King Charles the
Second came instead,
Revised their date and sought
another world:
I mean — not heaven but —
America.
A fervid stock, whose generous
hope embraced
The fortunes of mankind, not
stopping short

At rise of leather, or the fall of
gold,
Nor listening to the voices of the
time
As housewives listen to a
cackling hen,
With wonder whether she has
laid her egg
On their own nest-egg. Still they
did insist
Somewhat too wearisomely on
the joys
Of their Millennium, when coats
and hats
Would all be of one pattern,
books and songs
All fit for Sundays, and the
casual talk
As good as sermons preached
extempore.

And in Elias the ancestral zeal

Breathes strong as ever, only modified
By Transatlantic air and modern thought.
You could not pass him in the street and fail
To note his shoulders' long declivity,
Beard to the waist, swan-neck, and large pale eyes;
Or, when he lifts his hat, to mark his hair
Brushed back to show his great capacity —
A full grain's length at the angle of the brow
Proving him witty, while the shallower men
Only seem witty in their repartees.
Not that he's vain, but that his doctrine needs
The testimony of his frontal

lobe.
On all points he adopts the
latest views;
Takes for the key of universal
Mind
The " levitation " of stout
gentlemen;
Believes the Rappings are not
spirits' work,
But the Thought-atmosphere's,
a steam of brains
In correlated force of raps, as
proved
By motion, heat, and science
generally;
The spectrum, for example,
which has shown
The self-same metals in the sun
as here;
So the Thought-atmosphere is
everywhere:
High truths that glimmered
under other names

To ancient sages, whence good
scholarship
Applied to Eleusinian mysteries
—

The Vedas — Tripitaka —
Vendidad —
Might furnish weaker proof for
weaker minds
That Thought was rapping in the
hoary past,
And might have edified the
Greeks by raps
At the greater Dionysia, if their
ears
Had not been filled with
Sophoclean verse.
And when all Earth is vegetarian
—

When, lacking butchers,
quadrupeds die out,
And less Thought-atmosphere is

reabsorbed
By nerves of insects parasitical,
Those higher truths, seized now
by higher minds
But not expressed (the insects
hindering)
Will either flash out into
eloquence,
Or better still, be
comprehensible
By rappings simply, without
need of roots.

'Tis on this theme — the
vegetarian world —
That good Elias willingly
expands:
He loves to tell in mildly nasal
tones
And vowels stretched to suit the
widest views,
The future fortunes of our infant

Earth —
When it will be too full of
human kind
To have the room for wilder
animals.
Saith he, Sahara will be
populous
With families of gentlemen
retired
From commerce in more Central
Africa,
Who order coolness as we order
coal,
And have a lobe anterior strong
enough
To think away the sand-storms.
Science thus
Will leave no spot on this
terraqueous globe
Unfit to be inhabited by man,
The chief of animals: all meaner
brutes
Will have been smoked and

elbowed out of life.
No lions then shall lap Caffrarian
pools,
Or shake the Atlas with their
midnight roar:
Even the slow, slime-loving
crocodile,
The last of animals to take a
hint,
Will then retire for ever from a
scene
Where public feeling strongly
sets against him.
Fishes may lead carnivorous
lives obscure,
But must not dream of culinary
rank
Or being dished in good society.
Imagination in that distant age,
Aiming at fiction called
historical,
Will vainly try to reconstruct the
times

When it was men's
preposterous delight
To sit astride live horses, which
consumed
Materials for incalculable cakes;
When there were milkmaids
who drew milk from cows
With udders kept abnormal for
that end
Since the rude mythopoeic
period
Of Aryan dairymen, who did not
blush
To call their milkmaid and their
daughter one —
Helplessly gazing at the Milky
Way,
Nor dreaming of the astral
cocoa-nuts
Quite at the service of
posterity.
'Tis to be feared, though, that
the duller boys,

Much given to anachronisms
and nuts,
(Elias has confessed boys will be
boys)
May write a jockey for a
centaur, think
Europa's suitor was an Irish
bull,
Æsop a journalist who wrote up
Fox,
And Bruin a chief swindler upon
'Change.
Boys will be boys, but dogs will
all be moral,
With longer alimentary canals
Suited to diet vegetarian.
The uglier breeds will fade from
memory,
Or, being palaeontological,
Live but as portraits in large
learned books,
Distasteful to the feelings of an
age

Nourished on purest beauty.
Earth will hold
No stupid brutes, no cheerful
queernesses,
No naive cunning, grave
absurdity.
Wart-pigs with tender and
parental grunts,
Wombats much flattened as to
their contour,
Perhaps from too much crushing
in the ark,
But taking meekly that fatality;
The serious cranes, unstung by
ridicule;
Long-headed, short-legged,
solemn-looking curs,
(Wise, silent critics of a flippant
age);
The silly straddling foals, the
weak-brained geese
Hissing fallaciously at sound of
wheels —

All these rude products will have
disappeared
Along with every faulty human
type.
By dint of diet vegetarian
All will be harmony of hue and
line,
Bodies and minds all perfect,
limbs well-turned,
And talk quite free from aught
erroneous.
Thus far Elias in his seer's
mantle:
But at this climax in his
prophecy
My sinking spirits, fearing to be
swamped,
Urge me to speak. " High
prospects these, my friend,
Setting the weak carnivorous
brain astretch;
We will resume the thread
another day. "

" To-morrow, " cries Elias, " at this hour? "
" No, not to-morrow — I shall have a cold —
At least I feel some soreness — this endemic —
Good-bye. "
No tears are sadder than the smile
With which I quit Elias. Bitterly
I feel that every change upon this earth
Is bought with sacrifice. My yearnings fail
To reach that high apocalyptic mount
Which shows in bird's-eye view a perfect world,
Or enter warmly into other joys
Than those of faulty, struggling human kind.
That strain upon my soul's too feeble wing

Ends in ignoble floundering: I
fall
Into short-sighted pity for the
men
Who living in those perfect
future times
Will not know half the dear
imperfect things
That move my smiles and tears
— will never know
The fine old incongruities that
raise
My friendly laugh; the innocent
conceits
That like a needless eyeglass or
black patch
Give those who wear them
harmless happiness;
The twists and cracks in our
poor earthenware,
That touch me to more
conscious fellowship
(I am not myself the finest

Parian)
With my coevals. So poor Colin
Clout,
To whom raw onion gives
prospective zest,
Consoling hours of dampest
wintry work,
Could hardly fancy any regal
joys
Quite unimpregnate with the
onion's scent:
Perhaps his highest hopes are
not all clear
Of waftings from that energetic
bulb:
'Tis well that onion is not
heresy.
Speaking in parable, I am Colin
Clout.
A clinging flavour penetrates my
life —
My onion is imperfectness: I
cleave

To nature's blunders,
evanescent types
Which sages banish from
Utopia.
" Not worship beauty? " say
you. Patience, friend!
I worship in the temple with the
rest;
But by my hearth I keep a
sacred nook
For gnomes and dwarfs, duck-
footed waddling elves
Who stitched and hammered
for the weary man
In days of old. And in that piety
I clothe ungainly forms
inherited
From toiling generations, daily
bent
At desk, or plough, or loom, or
in the mine,
In pioneering labours for the
world.

Nay, I am apt when floundering
confused
From too rash flight, to grasp at
paradox,
And pity future men who will
not know
A keen experience with pity
blent,
The pathos exquisite of lovely
minds
Hid in harsh forms — not
penetrating them
Like fire divine within a common
bush
Which glows transfigured by the
heavenly guest,
So that men put their shoes off;
but encaged
Like a sweet child within some
thick-walled cell,
Who leaps and fails to hold the
window-bars,
But having shown a little

dimpled hand
Is visited thenceforth by tender
hearts
Whose eyes keep watch about
the prison walls.
A foolish, nay, a wicked
paradox!
For purest pity is the eye of love
Melting at sight of sorrow; and
to grieve
Because it sees no sorrow,
shows a love
Warped from its truer nature,
turned to love
Of merest habit, like the miser's
greed.
But I am Colin still: my
prejudice
Is for the flavour of my daily
food.
Not that I doubt the world is
growing still
As once it grew from Chaos and

from Night;
Or have a soul too shrunken for
the hope
Which dawned in human
breasts, a double morn,
With earliest watchings of the
rising light
Chasing the darkness; and
through many an age
Has raised the vision of a future
time
That stands an Angel with a face
all mild
Spearing the demon. I too rest
in faith
That man's perfection is the
crowning flower,
Toward which the urgent sap in
life's great tree
Is pressing, — seen in puny
blossoms now,
But in the world's great
morrows to expand

With broadest petal and with
deepest glow.

Yet, see the patched and
plodding citizen
Waiting upon the pavement
with the throng
While some victorious world-
hero makes
Triumphal entry, and the peal of
shouts
And flash of faces 'neath
uplifted hats
Run like a storm of joy along the
streets!
He says, " God bless him! "
almost with a sob,
As the great hero passes; he is
glad
The world holds mighty men
and mighty deeds;
The music stirs his pulses like

strong wine,
The moving splendour touches
him with awe —
'Tis glory shed around the
common weal,
And he will pay his tribute
willingly,
Though with the pennies earned
by sordid toil.
Perhaps the hero's deeds have
helped to bring
A time when every honest
citizen
Shall wear a coat unpatched.
And yet he feels
More easy fellowship with
neighbours there
Who look on too; and he will
soon relapse
From noticing the banners and
the steeds
To think with pleasure there is
just one bun

Left in his pocket, that may
serve to tempt
The wide-eyed lad, whose
weight is all too much
For that young mother's arms:
and then he falls
To dreamy picturing of sunny
days
When he himself was a small
big-cheeked lad
In some far village where no
heroes came,
And stood a listener 'twixt his
father's legs
In the warm fire-light, while the
old folk talked
And shook their heads and
looked upon the floor;
And he was puzzled, thinking life
was fine —
The bread and cheese so nice all
through the year
And Christmas sure to come. Oh

that good time!
He, could he choose, would
have those days again
And see the dear old-fashioned
things once more.
But soon the wheels and drums
have all passed by
And tramping feet are heard like
sudden rain:
The quiet startles our good
citizen;
He feels the child upon his arms,
and knows
He is with the people making
holiday
Because of hopes for better
days to come.
But Hope to him was like the
brilliant west
Telling of sunrise in a world
unknown,
And from that dazzling curtain
of bright hues

He turned to the familiar face of
fields
Lying all clear in the calm
morning land.
Maybe 'tis wiser not to fix a
lens
Too scrutinising on the glorious
times
When Barbarossa shall arise and
shake
His mountain, good King Arthur
come again,
And all the heroes of such giant
soul
That, living once to cheer
mankind with hope,
They had to sleep until the time
was ripe
For greater deeds to match their
greater thought.
Yet no! the earth yields nothing
more Divine
Than high prophetic vision —

than the Seer
Who fasting from man's meaner
joy beholds
The paths of beauteous order,
and constructs
A fairer type, to shame our low
content.
But prophecy is like potential
sound
Which turned to music seems a
voice sublime
From out the soul of light; but
turns to noise
In scrannel pipes, and makes all
ears averse.

The faith that life on earth is
being shaped
To glorious ends, that order,
justice, love
Mean man's completeness,
mean effect as sure

As roundness in the dew-drop
— that great faith
Is but the rushing and expanding
stream
Of thought, of feeling, fed by all
the past.
Our finest hope is finest
memory,
As they who love in age think
youth is blest
Because it has a life to fill with
love.
Full souls are double mirrors,
making still
An endless vista of fair things
before
Repeating things behind: so
faith is strong
Only when we are strong,
shrinks when we shrink.
It comes when music stirs us,
and the chords
Moving on some grand climax

shake our souls
With influx new that makes new
energies.
It comes in swellings of the
heart and tears
That rise at noble and at gentle
deeds —
At labours of the master-artist's
hand
Which, trembling, touches to a
finer end,
Trembling before an image seen
within.
It comes in moments of heroic
love,
Unjealous joy in joy not made
for us —
In conscious triumph of the
good within
Making us worship goodness
that rebukes.
Even our failures are a
prophecy,

Even our yearnings and our
bitter tears
After that fair and true we
cannot grasp;
As patriots who seem to die in
vain
Make liberty more sacred by
their pangs.

Presentiment of better things
on earth
Sweeps in with every force that
stirs our souls
To admiration, self-renouncing
love,
Or thoughts, like light, that bind
the world in one:
Sweeps like the sense of
vastness, when at night
We hear the roll and dash of
waves that break
Nearer and nearer with the

rushing tide,
Which rises to the level of the
cliff
Because the wide Atlantic rolls
behind
Throbbing respondent to the
far-off orbs.

Arion

Arion, whose melodic soul
Taught the dithyramb to roll
Like forest fires, and sing
Olympian suffering,

Had carried his diviner lore
From Corinth to the sister shore
Where Greece could largelier
be,
Branching o'er Italy.

Then weighted with his glorious
name
And bags of gold, aboard he
came
'Mid harsh seafaring men
To Corinth bound again.

The sailors eyed the bags and
thought:
" The gold is good, the man is
nought —
And who shall track the wave
That opens for his grave? "

With brawny arms and cruel
eyes
They press around him where
he lies
In sleep beside his lyre,
Hearing the Muses quire.

He waked and saw this wolf-
faced Death
Breaking the dream that filled
his breath
With inspiration strong
Of yet unchanted song.

" Take, take my gold and let me
live! "
He prayed, as kings do when
they give
Their all with royal will,
Holding born kingship still.

To rob the living they refuse,
One death or other he must
choose,
Either the watery pall
Or wounds and burial.

" My solemn robe then let me
don,
Give me high space to stand
upon,
That dying I may pour
A song unsung before. "

It pleased them well to grant
this prayer,
To hear for nought how it might
fare
With men who paid their gold
For what a poet sold.

In flowing stole, his eyes aglow
With inward fire, he neared the
prow
And took his god-like stand,
The cithara in hand.

The wolfish men all shrank
aloof,
And feared this singer might be
proof
Against their murderous power,
After his lyric hour.

But he, in liberty of song,
Fearless of death or other
wrong,
With full spondaic toll
Poured forth his mighty soul:

Poured forth the strain his
dream had taught,
A nome with lofty passion
fraught
Such as makes battles won
On fields of Marathon.

The last long vowels trembled
then
As awe within those wolfish
men:
They said, with mutual stare,
Some god was present there.

But lo! Arion leaped on high
Ready, his descant done, to die;
Not asking, " Is it well? "
Like a pierced eagle fell.

A College Breakfast-Party

Young Hamlet, not the
hesitating Dane,
But one named after him, who
lately strove
For honours at our English
Wittenberg, —
Blond, metaphysical, and
sensuous,
Questioning all things and yet
half convinced
Credulity were better; held
inert
'Twixt fascinations of all
opposites,
And half suspecting that the
mightiest soul
(Perhaps his own?) was union of
extremes,
Having no choice but choice of
everything:

As, drinking deep to-day for love
of wine,
To-morrow half a Brahmin,
scorning life
As mere illusion, yearning for
that True
Which has no qualities; another
day
Finding the fount of grace in
sacraments,
And purest reflex of the light
divine
In gem-bossed pyx and
broidered chasuble,
Resolved to wear no stockings
and to fast
With arms extended, waiting
ecstasy;
But getting cramps instead, and
needing change,
A would-be pagan next: —
Young Hamlet sat
A guest with five of somewhat

riper age
At breakfast with Horatio, a
friend
With few opinions, but of
faithful heart,
Quick to detect the fibrous
spreading roots
Of character that feed men's
theories,
Yet cloaking weaknesses with
charity
And ready in all service save
rebuke.

With ebb of breakfast and the
cider-cup
Came high debate: the others
seated there
Were Osric, spinner of fine
sentences,
A delicate insect creeping over
life
Feeding on molecules of floral

breath,
And weaving gossamer to trap
the sun;
Laertes ardent, rash, and
radical;
Discursive Rosencranz, grave
Guildenstern,
And he for whom the social
meal was made —
The polished priest, a tolerant
listener,
Disposed to give a hearing to
the lost,
And breakfast with them ere
they went below.

From alpine metaphysic glaciers
first
The talk sprang copious; the
themes were old,
But so is human breath, so
infant eyes,
The daily nurslings of creative

light.
Small words held mighty
meanings: Matter, Force,
Self, Not-self, Being, Seeming,
Space and Time —
Plebeian toilers on the dusty
road
Of daily traffic, turned to Genii
And cloudy giants darkening sun
and moon.
Creation was reversed in human
talk:
None said, " Let Darkness be, "
but Darkness was;
And in it weltered with Teutonic
ease,
An argumentative Leviathan,
Blowing cascades from out his
element,
The thunderous Rosencranz, till
" Truce, I beg! "
Said Osric, with nice accent. " I
abhor

That battling of the ghosts, that
strife of terms
For utmost lack of colour, form,
and breath,
That tasteless squabbling called
Philosophy:
As if a blue-winged butterfly
afloat
For just three days above the
Italian fields,
Instead of sipping at the heart
of flowers,
Poising in sunshine, fluttering
towards its bride,
Should fast and speculate,
considering
What were if it were not? or
what now is
Instead of that which seems to
be itself?
Its deepest wisdom surely were
to be
A sipping, marrying, blue-

winged butterfly;
Since utmost speculation on
itself
Were but a three days' living of
worse sort —
A bruising struggle all within the
bounds
Of butterfly existence. "
" I protest, "
Burst in Laertes, " against
arguments
That start with calling me a
butterfly,
A bubble, spark, or other
metaphor
Which carries your conclusions
as a phrase
In quibbling law will carry
property.
Put a thin sucker for my human
lips
Fed at a mother's breast, who
now needs food

That I will earn for her; put
bubbles blown
From frothy thinking, for the
joy, the love,
The wants, the pity, and the
fellowship
(The ocean deeps I might say,
were I bent
On bandying metaphors) that
make a man —
Why, rhetoric brings within your
easy reach
Conclusions worthy of — a
butterfly.
The universe, I hold, is no
charade,
No acted pun unriddled by a
word,
Nor pain a decimal diminishing
With hocus-pocus of a dot or
nought.
For those who know it, pain is
solely pain:

Not any letters of the alphabet
Wrought syllogistically pattern-
wise,
Nor any cluster of fine images,
Nor any missing of their figured
dance
By blundering molecules.
Analysis
May show you the right physic
for the ill,
Teaching the molecules to find
their dance,
But spare me your analogies,
that hold
Such insight as the figure of a
crow
And bar of music put to signify
A crowbar. "
Said the Priest, " There I agree
—
Would add that sacramental
grace is grace
Which to be known must first be

felt, with all
The strengthening influxes that
come by prayer.
I note this passingly — would
not delay
The conversation's tenor, save
to hint
That taking stand with
Rosencranz one sees
Final equivalence of all we
name
Our Good and Ill — their
difference meanwhile
Being inborn prejudice that
plumps you down
An Ego, brings a weight into
your scale
Forcing a standard. That
resistless weight
Obstinate, irremovable by
thought,
Persisting through disproof, an
ache, a need

That spaceless stays where
sharp analysis
Has shown a plenum filled
without it — what
If this, to use your phrase, were
just that Being
Not looking solely, grasping
from the dark,
Weighing the difference you call
Ego? This
Gives you persistence, regulates
the flux
With strict relation rooted in the
All.
Who is he of your late
philosophers
Takes the true name of Being to
be Will?
I — nay, the Church objects
nought, is content:
Reason has reached its utmost
negative,
Physic and metaphysic meet in

the inane
And backward shrink to intense
prejudice,
Making their absolute and
homogene
A loaded relative, a choice to be
Whatever is — supposed: a
What is not.
The Church demands no more,
has standing room
And basis for her doctrine: this
(no more) —
That the strong bias which we
name the Soul,
Though fed and clad by
dissoluble waves,
Has antecedent quality, and
rules
By veto or consent the strife of
thought,
Making arbitrament that we call
faith. "

Here was brief silence, till young
Hamlet spoke.
" I crave direction, Father, how
to know
The sign of that imperative
whose right
To sway my act in face of
thronging doubts
Were an oracular gem in price
beyond
Urim and Thummim lost to
Israel.
That bias of the soul, that
conquering die
Loaded with golden emphasis of
Will —
How find it where resolve, once
made, becomes
The rash exclusion of an
opposite
Which draws the stronger as I
turn aloof. "

" I think I hear a bias in your words, "
The Priest said mildly, — " that strong natural bent
Which we call hunger. What more positive
Than appetite? — of spirit or of flesh,
I care not — " sense of need" were truer phrase.
You hunger for authoritative right,
And yet discern no difference of tones,
No weight of rod that marks imperial rule?
Laertes granting, I will put your case
In analogic form: the doctors hold
Hunger which gives no relish — save caprice
That tasting venison fancies

mellow pears —
A symptom of disorder, and prescribe
Strict discipline. Were I physician here
I would prescribe that exercise of soul
Which lies in full obedience: you ask,
Obedience to what? The answer lies
Within the word itself; for how obey
What has no rule, asserts no absolute claim?
Take inclination, taste — why, that is you,
No rule above you. Science, reasoning
On nature's order — they exist and move
Solely by disputation, hold no pledge

Of final consequence, but push
the swing
Where Epicurus and the Stoic
sit
In endless see-saw. One
authority,
And only one, says simply this,
Obey:
Place yourself in that current
(test it so!)
Of spiritual order where at least
Lies promise of a high
communion
A Head informing members, Life
that breathes
With gift of forces over and
above
The plus of arithmetic
interchange.
" The Church too has a body,"
you object,
" Can be dissected, put beneath
the lens

And shown the merest
continuity
Of all existence else beneath the
sun."
I grant you; but the lens will not
disprove
A presence which eludes it. Take
your wit,
Your highest passion, widest-
reaching thought:
Show their conditions if you will
or can,
But though you saw the final
atom-dance
Making each molecule that
stands for sign
Of love being present, where is
still your love?
How measure that, how certify
its weight?
And so I say, the body of the
Church
Carries a Presence, promises

and gifts
Never disproved — whose
argument is found
In lasting failure of the search
elsewhere
For what it holds to satisfy
man's need.
But I grow lengthy: my excuse
must be
Your question, Hamlet, which
has probed right through
To the pith of our belief. And I
have robbed
Myself of pleasure as a listener.
'Tis noon, I see; and my
appointment stands
For half-past twelve with
Voltimand. Good-bye. "

Brief parting, brief regret —
sincere, but quenched
In fumes of best Havannah,
which consoles

For lack of other certitude. Then said,
Mildly sarcastic, quiet Guildenstern:
" I marvel how the Father gave new charm
To weak conclusions: I was half convinced
The poorest reasoner made the finest man,
And held his logic lovelier for its limp. "

" I fain would hear, " said Hamlet, " how you find
A stronger footing than the Father gave.
How base your self-resistance save on faith
In some invisible Order, higher Right
Than changing impulse. What does Reason bid?

To take a fullest rationality
What offers best solution: so
the Church.
Science, detecting hydrogen
aflame
Outside our firmament, leaves
mystery
Whole and untouched beyond;
nay, in our blood
And in the potent atoms of each
germ
The Secret lives — envelops,
penetrates
Whatever sense perceives or
thought divines.
Science, whose soul is
explanation, halts
With hostile front at mystery.
The Church
Takes mystery as her empire,
brings its wealth
Of possibility to fill the void
'Twixt contradictions —

warrants so a faith
Defying sense and all its ruthless
train
Of arrogant " Therefores."
Science with her lens
Dissolves the Forms that made
the other half
Of all our love, which
thenceforth widowed lives
To gaze with maniac stare at
what is not.
The Church explains not,
governs — feeds resolve
By vision fraught with heart-
experience
And human yearning. "
" Ay, " said Guildenstern.
With friendly nod, " the Father, I
can see,
Has caught you up in his air-
chariot.
His thought takes rainbow-
bridges, out of reach

By solid obstacles, evaporates
The coarse and common into
subtilties,
Insists that what is real in the
Church
Is something out of evidence,
and begs
(Just in parenthesis) you'll never
mind
What stares you in the face and
bruises you.
Why, by his method I could
justify
Each superstition and each
tyranny
That ever rode upon the back of
man,
Pretending fitness for his sole
defence
Against life's evil. How can
aught subsist
That holds no theory of gain or
good?

Despots with terror in their red
right hand
Must argue good to helpers and
themselves,
Must let submission hold a core
of gain
To make their slaves choose life.
Their theory,
Abstracting inconvenience of
racks,
Whip-lashes, dragonnades and
all things coarse
Inherent in the fact or concrete
mass,
Presents the pure idea —
utmost good
Secured by Order only to be
found
In strict subordination,
hierarchy
Of forces where, by nature's
law, the strong
Has rightful empire, rule of

weaker proved
Mere dissolution. What can you
object?
The Inquisition — if you turn
away
From narrow notice how the
scent of gold
Has guided sense of damning
heresy —
The Inquisition is sublime, is
love
Hindering the spread of poison
in men's souls:
The flames are nothing: only
smaller pain
To hinder greater, or the pain of
one
To save the many, such as
throbs at heart
Of every system born into the
world.
So of the Church as high
communion

Of Head with members, fount of
spirit force
Beyond the calculus, and
carrying proof
In her sole power to satisfy
man's need:
That seems ideal truth as clear
as lines
That, necessary though invisible,
trace
The balance of the planets and
the sun —
Until I find a hitch in that last
claim.
" To satisfy man's need." Sir,
that depends:
We settle first the measure of
man's need
Before we grant capacity to fill.
John, James, or Thomas, you
may satisfy:
But since you choose ideals I
demand

Your Church shall satisfy ideal
man,
His utmost reason and his
utmost love.
And say these rest a-hungered
— find no scheme
Content them both, but hold
the world accursed,
A Calvary where Reason mocks
at Love,
And Love forsaken sends out
orphan cries
Hopeless of answer; still the
soul remains
Larger, diviner than your half-
way Church,
Which racks your reason into
false consent,
And soothes your Love with
sops of selfishness. "
" There I am with you, " cried
Laertes. " What
To me are any dictates, though

they came
With thunders from the Mount,
if still within
I see a higher Right, a higher
Good
Compelling love and worship?
Though the earth
Held force electric to discern
and kill
Each thinking rebel — what is
martyrdom
But death-defying utterance of
belief,
Which being mine remains my
truth supreme
Though solitary as the throb of
pain
Lying outside the pulses of the
world?
Obedience is good: ay, but to
what?
And for what ends? For say that
I rebel

Against your rule as devilish, or
as rule
Of thunder-guiding powers that
deny
Man's highest benefit: rebellion
then
Were strict obedience to
another rule
Which bids me flout your
thunder. "
" Lo you now! "
Said Osric, delicately, " how you
come,
Laertes mine, with all your
warring zeal
As Python-slayer of the present
age —
Cleansing all social swamps by
darting rays
Of dubious doctrine, hot with
energy
Of private judgment and disgust
for doubt —

To state my thesis, which you most abhor
When sung in Daphnis-notes beneath the pines
To gentle rush of waters. Your belief —
In essence what is it but simply Taste?
I urge with you exemption from all claims
That come from other than my proper will,
An Ultimate within to balance yours,
A solid meeting you, excluding you,
Till you show fuller force by entering
My spiritual space and crushing Me
To a subordinate complement of You:
Such ultimate must stand alike

for all.
Preach your crusade, then: all
will join who like
The hurly-burly of aggressive
creeds;
Still your unpleasant Ought,
your itch to choose
What grates upon the sense, is
simply Taste,
Differs, I think, from mine
(permit the word,
Discussion forces it) in being
bad. "

The tone was too polite to
breed offence,
Showing a tolerance of what
was " bad "
Becoming courtiers. Louder
Rosencranz
Took up the ball with rougher
movement, wont
To show contempt for doting

reasoners
Who hugged some reasons with
a preference,
As warm Laertes did: he gave
five puffs
Intolerantly sceptical, then said,
" Your human good, which you
would make supreme,
How do you know it? Has it
shown its face
In adamantine type, with
features clear,
As this republic, or that
monarchy?
As federal grouping, or
municipal?
Equality, or finely shaded lines
Of social difference? ecstatic
whirl
And draught intense of
passionate joy and pain,
Or sober self-control that
starves its youth

And lives to wonder what the
world calls joy?
Is it in sympathy that shares
men's pangs
Or in cool brains that can
explain them well?
Is it in labour or in laziness?
In training for the tug of rivalry
To be admired, or in the
admiring soul?
In risk or certitude? In battling
rage
And hardy challenges of Protean
luck,
Or in a sleek and rural apathy
Full fed with sameness? Pray
define your Good
Beyond rejection by majority;
Next, how it may subsist
without the Ill
Which seems its only outline.
Show a world
Of pleasure not resisted; or a

world
Of pressure equalised, yet
various
In action formative; for that will
serve
As illustration of your human
good —
Which at its perfecting (your
goal of hope)
Will not be straight extinct, or
fall to sleep
In the deep bosom of the
Unchangeable.
What will you work for, then,
and call it good
With full and certain vision —
good for aught
Save partial ends which happen
to be yours?
How will you get your stringency
to bind
Thought or desire in
demonstrated tracks

Which are but waves within a
balanced whole?
Is " relative" the magic word
that turns
Your flux mercurial of good to
gold?
Why, that analysis at which you
rage
As anti-social force that sweeps
you down
The world in one cascade of
molecules,
Is brother " relative" — and
grins at you
Like any convict whom you
thought to send
Outside society, till this
enlarged
And meant New England and
Australia too.
The Absolute is your shadow,
and the space
Which you say might be real

were you milled
To curves pellicular, the thinnest thin,
Equation of no thickness, is still you. "

" Abstracting all that makes him clubbable, "
Horatio interposed. But Rosencranz,
Deaf as the angry turkey-cock whose ears
Are plugged by swollen tissues when he scolds
At men's pretensions: " Pooh, your " Relative"
Shuts you in, hopeless, with your progeny
As in a Hunger-tower; your social good,
Like other deities by turn supreme,
Is transient reflex of a

prejudice,
Anthology of causes and effects
To suit the mood of fanatics
who lead
The mood of tribes or nations. I
admit
If you could show a sword, nay,
chance of sword
Hanging conspicuous to their
inward eyes
With edge so constant
threatening as to sway
All greed and lust by terror; and
a law
Clear-writ and proven as the law
supreme
Which that dread sword
enforces — then your Right,
Duty, or social Good, were it
once brought
To common measure with the
potent law,
Would dip the scale, would put

unchanging marks
Of wisdom or of folly on each
deed,
And warrant exhortation. Until
then,
Where is your standard or
criterion?
" What always, everywhere, by
all men" — why,
That were but Custom, and your
system needs
Ideals never yet incorporate,
The imminent doom of Custom.
Can you find
Appeal beyond the sentience in
each man?
Frighten the blind with
scarecrows? raise an awe
Of things unseen where
appetite commands
Chambers of imagery in the
soul
At all its avenues? — You chant

your hymns
To Evolution, on your altar lay
A sacred egg called Progress:
have you proved
A Best unique where all is
relative,
And where each change is loss
as well as gain?
The age of healthy Saurians,
well supplied
With heat and prey, will balance
well enough
A human age where maladies
are strong
And pleasures feeble; wealth a
monster gorged
Mid hungry populations;
intellect
Aproned in laboratories, bent
on proof
That this is that and both are
good for nought
Save feeding error through a

weary life;
While Art and Poesy struggle
like poor ghosts
To hinder cock-crow and the
dreadful light,
Lurking in darkness and the
charnel-house,
Or like two stalwart greybeards,
imbecile
With limbs still active, playing at
belief
That hunt the slipper, foot-ball,
hide-and-seek,
Are sweetly merry, donning
pinafores
And lisping emulously in their
speech.
O human race! Is this then all
thy gain? —
Working at disproof, playing at
belief,
Debate on causes, distaste of
effects,

Power to transmute all
elements, and lack
Of any power to sway the fatal
skill
And make thy lot aught else
than rigid doom?
The Saurians were better. —
Guildenstern,
Pass me the taper. Still the
human curse
Has mitigation in the best cigars.
"

Then swift Laertes, not without
a glare
Of leonine wrath, " I thank thee
for that word:
That one confession, were I
Socrates,
Should force you onward till you
ran your head
At your own image — flatly gave
the lie

To all your blasphemy of that
human good
Which bred and nourished you
to sit at ease
And learnedly deny it. Say the
world
Groans ever with the pangs of
doubtful births:
Say, life's a poor donation at the
best —
Wisdom a yearning after
nothingness —
Nature's great vision and the
thrill supreme
Of thought-fed passion but a
weary play —
I argue not against you. Who
can prove
Wit to be witty when with
deeper ground
Dulness intuitive declares wit
dull?
If life is worthless to you — why,

it is.
You only know how little love
you feel
To give you fellowship, how
little force
Responsive to the quality of
things.
Then end your life, throw off the
unsought yoke.
If not — if you remain to taste
cigars,
Choose racy diction, perorate at
large
With tacit scorn of meaner men
who win
No wreath or tripos — then
admit at least
A possible Better in the seeds of
earth;
Acknowledge debt to that
laborious life
Which, sifting evermore the
mingled seeds,

Testing the Possible with patient
skill,
And daring ill in presence of a
good
For futures to inherit, made
your lot
One you would choose rather
than end it, nay,
Rather than, say, some twenty
million lots
Of fellow-Britons toiling all to
make
That nation, that community,
whereon
You feed and thrive and talk
philosophy.
I am no optimist whose faith
must hang
On hard pretence that pain is
beautiful
And agony explained for men at
ease
By virtue's exercise in pitying it.

But this I hold: that he who
takes one gift
Made for him by the hopeful
work of man,
Who tastes sweet bread, walks
where he will unarmed,
His shield and warrant the
invisible law,
Who owns a hearth and
household charities,
Who clothes his body and his
sentient soul
With skill and thoughts of men,
and yet denies
A human good worth toiling for,
is cursed
With worse negation than the
poet feigned
In Mephistopheles. The Devil
spins
His wire-drawn argument
against all good
With sense of brimstone as his

private lot,
And never drew a solace from
the Earth. "

Laertes fuming paused, and
Guildenstern
Took up with cooler skill the
fusillade:
" I meet your deadliest
challenge, Rosencranz: —
Where get, you say, a binding
law, a rule
Enforced by sanction, an Ideal
throned
With thunder in its hand? I
answer, there
Whence every faith and rule has
drawn its force
Since human consciousness
awaking owned
An Outward, whose
unconquerable sway
Resisted first and then subdued

desire
By pressure of the dire
Impossible
Urging to possible ends the
active soul
And shaping so its terror and its
love.
Why, you have said it — threats
and promises
Depend on each man's
sentience for their force:
All sacred rules, imagined or
revealed,
Can have no form or potency
apart
From the percipient and
emotive mind.
God, duty, love, submission,
fellowship,
Must first be framed in man, as
music is,
Before they live outside him as a
law.

And still they grow and shape
themselves anew,
With fuller concentration in
their life
Of inward and of outward
energies
Blending to make the last result
called Man,
Which means, not this or that
philosopher
Looking through beauty into
blankness, not
The swindler who has sent his
fruitful lie
By the last telegram: it means
the tide
Of needs reciprocal, toil, trust,
and love —
The surging multitude of human
claims
Which make " a presence not to
be put by"
Above the horizon of the

general soul.
Is inward Reason shrunk to
subtleties,
And inward wisdom pining
passion-starved? —
The outward Reason has the
world in store,
Regenerates passion with the
stress of want,
Regenerates knowledge with
discovery,
Shows sly rapacious Self a
blunderer,
Widens dependence, knits the
social whole
In sensible relation more
defined.
Do Boards and dirty-handed
millionaires
Govern the planetary system?
— sway
The pressure of the Universe?
— decide

That man henceforth shall
retrogress to ape,
Emptied of every sympathetic
thrill
The All has wrought in him?
dam up henceforth
The flood of human claims as
private force
To turn their wheels and make a
private hell
For fish-pond to their mercantile
domain?
What are they but a parasitic
growth
On the vast real and ideal world
Of man and nature blent in one
divine?
Why, take your closing dirge —
say evil grows
And good is dwindling; science
mere decay,
Mere dissolution of ideal
wholes

Which through the ages past
alone have made
The earth and firmament of
human faith;
Say, the small arc of Being we
call man
Is near its mergence, what
seems growing life
Nought but a hurrying change
towards lower types,
The ready rankness of
degeneracy.
Well, they who mourn for the
world's dying good
May take their common sorrows
for a rock,
On it erect religion and a
church,
A worship, rites, and passionate
piety —
The worship of the Best though
crucified
And God-forsaken in its dying

pangs;
The sacramental rites of
fellowship
In common woe; visions that
purify
Through admiration and
despairing love
Which keep their spiritual life
intact
Beneath the murderous clutches
of disproof
And feed a martyr-strength. "

" Religion high! "
(Rosencranz here) " but with
communicants
Few as the cedars upon
Lebanon —
A child might count them. What
the world demands
Is faith coercive of the
multitude. "

" Tush, Guildenstern, you
granted him too much, "
Burst in Laertes; " I will never
grant
One inch of law to feeble
blasphemies
Which hold no higher ratio to
life —
Full vigorous human life that
peopled earth
And wrought and fought and
loved and bravely died —
Than the sick morning glooms of
debauchees.
Old nations breed old children,
wizened babes
Whose youth is languid and
incredulous,
Weary of life without the will to
die;
Their passions visionary
appetites
Of bloodless spectres wailing

that the world
For lack of substance slips from
out their grasp;
Their thoughts the withered
husks of all things dead,
Holding no force of germs
instinct with life,
Which never hesitates but
moves and grows.
Yet hear them boast in screams
their godlike ill,
Excess of knowing! Fie on you,
Rosencranz!
You lend your brains and fine-
dividing tongue
For bass-notes to this shrivelled
crudity,
This immature decrepitude that
strains
To fill our ears and claim the
prize of strength
For mere unmanliness. Out on
them all! —

Wits, puling minstrels, and
philosophers,
Who living softly prate of
suicide,
And suck the commonwealth to
feed their ease
While they vent epigrams and
threnodies,
Mocking or wailing all the eager
work
Which makes that public store
whereon they feed.
Is wisdom flattened sense and
mere distaste?
Why, any superstition warm
with love,
Inspired with purpose, wild with
energy
That streams resistless through
its ready frame,
Has more of human truth within
its life
Than souls that look through

colour into nought, —
Whose brain, too
unimpassioned for delight,
Has feeble ticklings of a vanity
Which finds the universe
beneath its mark,
And scorning the blue heavens
as merely blue
Can only say, " What then?" —
pre-eminent
In wondrous want of likeness to
their kind,
Founding that worship of
sterility
Whose one supreme is
vacillating Will
Which makes the Light, then
says " 'Twere better not." "

Here rash Laertes brought his
Handel-strain
As of some angry Polypheme, to
pause;

And Osric, shocked at ardours
out of taste,
Relieved the audience with a
tenor voice
And delicate delivery.
" For me,
I range myself in line with
Rosencranz
Against all schemes, religious or
profane,
That flaunt a Good as pretext
for a lash
To flog us all who have the
better taste,
Into conformity, requiring me
At peril of the thong and sharp
disgrace
To care how mere Philistines
pass their lives;
Whether the English pauper-
total grows
From one to two before the
noughts; how far

Teuton will outbreed Roman; if
the class
Of proletaires will make a
federal band
To bind all Europe and America,
Throw, in their wrestling, every
government,
Snatch the world's purse and
keep the guillotine:
Or else (admitting these are
casualties)
Driving my soul with scientific
hail
That shuts the landscape out
with particles;
Insisting that the Palingenesis
Means telegraphs and measure
of the rate
At which the stars move —
nobody knows where.
So far, my Rosencranz, we are at
one.
But not when you blaspheme

the life of Art,
The sweet perennial youth of
Poesy,
Which asks no logic but its
sensuous growth,
No right but loveliness; which
fearless strolls
Betwixt the burning mountain
and the sea,
Reckless of earthquake and the
lava stream,
Filling its hour with beauty. It
knows nought
Of bitter strife, denial, grim
resolve,
Sour resignation, busy
emphasis
Of fresh illusions named the
new-born True,
Old Error's latest child; but as a
lake
Images all things, yet within its
depths

Dreams them all lovelier —
thrills with sound
And makes a harp of plenteous
liquid chords —
So Art or Poesy: we its votaries
Are the Olympians, fortunately
born
From the elemental mixture; 'tis
our lot
To pass more swiftly than the
Delian God,
But still the earth breaks into
flowers for us,
And mortal sorrows when they
reach our ears
Are dying falls to melody divine.
Hatred, war, vice, crime, sin,
those human storms,
Cyclones, floods, what you will
— outbursts of force —
Feed art with contrast, give the
grander touch
To the master's pencil and the

poet's song,

Serve as Vesuvian fires or navies tossed

On yawning waters, which when viewed afar

Deepen the calm sublime of those choice souls

Who keep the heights of poesy and turn

A fleckless mirror to the various world,

Giving its many-named and fitful flux

An imaged, harmless, spiritual life,

With pure selection, native to art's frame,

Of beauty only, save its minor scale

Of ill and pain to give the ideal joy

A keener edge. This is a mongrel globe;

All finer being wrought from its
coarse earth
Is but accepted privilege: what
else
Your boasted virtue, which
proclaims itself
A good above the average
consciousness?
Nature exists by partiality
(Each planet's poise must carry
two extremes
With verging breadths of minor
wretchedness):
We are her favourites and
accept our wings.
For your accusal, Rosencranz,
that art
Shares in the dread and
weakness of the time,
I hold it null; since art or poesy
pure,
Being blameless by all standards
save her own,

Takes no account of modern or
antique
In morals, science, or
philosophy:
No dull elenchus makes a yoke
for her,
Whose law and measure are the
sweet consent
Of sensibilities that move apart
From rise or fall of systems,
states or creeds —
Apart from what Philistines call
man's weal. "

" Ay, we all know those votaries
of the Muse
Ravished with singing till they
quite forgot
Their manhood, sang, and
gaped, and took no food,
Then died of emptiness, and for
reward
Lived on as grasshoppers " —

Laertes thus:
But then he checked himself as
one who feels
His muscles dangerous, and
Guildenstern
Filled up the pause with calmer
confidence.

" You use your wings, my Osric,
poise yourself
Safely outside all reach of
argument,
Then dogmatise at will (a
method known
To ancient women and
philosophers,
Nay, to Philistines whom you
most abhor);
Else, could an arrow reach you, I
should ask
Whence came taste, beauty,
sensibilities
Refined to preference

infallible?
Doubtless, ye're gods — these
odours ye inhale,
A sacrificial scent. But how, I
pray,
Are odours made, if not by
gradual change
Of sense or substance? Is your
beautiful
A seedless, rootless flower, or
has it grown
With human growth, which
means the rising sum
Of human struggle, order,
knowledge? — sense
Trained to a fuller record, more
exact —
To truer guidance of each
passionate force?
Get me your roseate flesh
without the blood;
Get fine aromas without
structure wrought

From simpler being into
manifold:
Then and then only flaunt your
Beautiful
As what can live apart from
thought, creeds, states,
Which mean life's structure.
Osric, I beseech —
The infallible should be more
catholic —
Join in a war-dance with the
cannibals,
Hear Chinese music, love a face
tattooed,
Give adoration to a pointed
skull,
And think the Hindu Siva looks
divine:
'Tis art, 'tis poesy. Say, you
object:
How came you by that lofty
dissidence,
If not through changes in the

social man
Widening his consciousness
from Here and Now
To larger wholes beyond the
reach of sense;
Controlling to a fuller harmony
The thrill of passion and the rule
of fact;
And paling false ideals in the
light
Of full-rayed sensibilities which
blend
Truth and desire? Taste, beauty,
what are they
But the soul's choice towards
perfect bias wrought
By finer balance of a fuller
growth —
Sense brought to subtlest
metamorphosis
Through love, thought, joy —
the general human store
Which grows from all life's

functions? As the plant
Holds its corolla, purple,
delicate,
Solely as outflush of that
energy
Which moves transformingly in
root and branch. "

Guildenstern paused, and
Hamlet quivering
Since Osric spoke, in transit
imminent
From catholic striving into
laxity,
Ventured his word. " Seems to
me, Guildenstern,
Your argument, though
shattering Osric's point
That sensibilities can move
apart
From social order, yet has not
annulled
His thesis that the life of poesy

(Admitting it must grow from
out the whole)
Has separate functions, a
transfigured realm
Freed from the rigours of the
practical,
Where what is hidden from the
grosser world —
Stormed down by roar of
engines and the shouts
Of eager concourse — rises
beauteous
As voice of water-drops in
sapphire caves;
A realm where finest spirits
have free sway
In exquisite selection,
uncontrolled
By hard material necessity
Of cause and consequence. For
you will grant
The Ideal has discoveries which
ask

No test, no faith, save that we
joy in them:
A new-found continent, with
spreading lands
Where pleasure charters all,
where virtue, rank,
Use, right, and truth have but
one name, Delight.
Thus Art's creations, when
etherealised
To least admixture of the
grosser fact
Delight may stamp as highest. "
" Possible! "
Said Guildenstern, with touch of
weariness,
" But then we might dispute of
what is gross,
What high, what low. "
" Nay, " said Laertes, " ask
The mightiest makers who have
reigned, still reign
Within the ideal realm. See if

their thought
Be drained of practice and the
thick warm blood
Of hearts that beat in action
various
Through the wide drama of the
struggling world.
Good-bye, Horatio. "

Each now said " Good-bye. "
Such breakfast, such beginning
of the day
Is more than half the whole. The
sun was hot
On southward branches of the
meadow elms,
The shadows slowly farther
crept and veered
Like changing memories, and
Hamlet strolled
Alone and dubious on the
empurpled path
Between the waving grasses of

new June
Close by the stream where well-compacted boats
Were moored or moving with a lazy creak
To the soft dip of oars. All sounds were light
As tiny silver bells upon the robes
Of hovering silence. Birds made twitterings
That seemed but Silence self o'erfull of love.
'Twas invitation all to sweet repose;
And Hamlet, drowsy with the mingled draughts
Of cider and conflicting sentiments,
Chose a green couch and watched with half-closed eyes
The meadow-road, the stream and dreamy lights,

Until they merged themselves in
sequence strange
With undulating ether, time, the
soul,
The will supreme, the individual
claim,
The social Ought, the lyrist's
liberty,
Democritus, Pythagoras, in talk
With Anselm, Darwin, Comte,
and Schopenhauer,
The poets rising slow from out
their tombs
Summoned as arbiters — that
border-world
Of dozing, ere the sense is fully
locked.

And then he dreamed a dream
so luminous
He woke (he says) convinced;
but what it taught
Withholds as yet. Perhaps those

graver shades
Admonished him that visions
told in haste
Part with their virtues to the
squandering lips
And leave the soul in wider
emptiness.

The Death Of Moses

Moses, who spake with God as
with his friend,
And ruled his people with the
twofold power
Of wisdom that can dare and
still be meek,
Was writing his last word, the
sacred name
Unutterable of that Eternal Will
Which was and is and evermore
shall be.
Yet was his task not finished, for
the flock
Needed its shepherd and the
life-taught sage
Leaves no successor; but to
chosen men,
The rescuers and guides of
Israel,
A death was given called the

Death of Grace,
Which freed them from the
burden of the flesh
But left them rulers of the
multitude
And loved companions of the
lonely. This
Was God's last gift to Moses,
this the hour
When soul must part from self
and be but soul.

God spake to Gabriel, the
messenger
Of mildest death that draws the
parting life
Gently, as when a little rosy
child
Lifts up its lips from off the bowl
of milk
And so draws forth a curl that
dipped its gold
In the soft white—thus Gabriel

draws the soul.
"Go bring the soul of Moses
unto me!"
And the awe-stricken angel
answered, "Lord,
How shall I dare to take his life
who lives
Sole of his kind, not to be
likened once
In all the generations of the
earth?"

Then God called Michaël, him of
pensive brow
Snow-vest and flaming sword,
who knows and acts:
"Go bring the spirit of Moses
unto me!"
But Michaël with such grief as
angels feel,
Loving the mortals whom they
succour, pled:
"Almighty, spare me; it was I

who taught
Thy servant Moses; he is part of me
As I of thy deep secrets,
knowing them."

Then God called Zamaël, the terrible,
The angel of fierce death, of agony
That comes in battle and in pestilence
Remorseless, sudden or with lingering throes.
And Zamaël, his raiment and broad wings
Blood-tinctured, the dark lustre of his eyes
Shrouding the red, fell like the gathering night
Before the prophet. But that radiance
Won from the heavenly

presence in the mount
Gleamed on the prophet's brow
and dazzling pierced
Its conscious opposite: the angel
turned
His murky gaze aloof and inly
said:
"An angel this, deathless to
angel's stroke."

But Moses felt the subtly
nearing dark:—
"Who art thou? and what wilt
thou?" Zamaël then:
"I am God's reaper; through the
fields of life
I gather ripened and unripened
souls
Both willing and unwilling. And I
come
Now to reap thee." But Moses
cried,
Firm as a seer who waits the

trusted sign:
"Reap thou the fruitless plant
and common herb—
Not him who from the womb
was sanctified
To teach the law of purity and
love."
And Zamaël baffled from his
errand fled.

But Moses, pausing, in the air
serene
Heard now that mystic whisper,
far yet near,
The all-penetrating Voice, that
said to him,
"Moses, the hour is come and
thou must die."
"Lord, I obey; but thou
rememberest
How thou, Ineffable, didst take
me once
Within thy orb of light

untouched by death."
Then the voice answered, "Be
no more afraid:
With me shall be thy death and
burial."
So Moses waited, ready now to
die.

And the Lord came, invisible as a
thought,
Three angels gleaming on his
secret track,
Prince Michaël, Zamaël, Gabriel,
charged to guard
The soul-forsaken body as it fell
And bear it to the hidden
sepulchre
Denied for ever to the search of
man.
And the Voice said to Moses:
"Close thine eyes."
He closed them. "Lay thine hand
upon thine heart,

And draw thy feet together." He
obeyed.
And the Lord said, "O spirit!
child of mine!
A hundred years and twenty
thou hast dwelt
Within this tabernacle wrought
of clay.
This is the end: come forth and
flee to heaven."

But the grieved soul with
plaintive pleading cried,
"I love this body with a clinging
love:
The courage fails me, Lord, to
part from it."

"O child, come forth! for thou
shalt dwell with me
About the immortal throne
where seraphs joy
In growing vision and in growing

love."

Yet hesitating, fluttering, like
the bird
With young wing weak and
dubious, the soul
Stayed. But behold! upon the
death-dewed lips
A kiss descended, pure,
unspeakable—
The bodiless Love without
embracing Love
That lingered in the body, drew
it forth
With heavenly strength and
carried it to heaven.

But now beneath the sky the
watchers all,
Angels that keep the homes of
Israel
Or on high purpose wander o'er
the world

Leading the Gentiles, felt a dark
eclipse:
The greatest ruler among men
was gone.
And from the westward sea was
heard a wail,
A dirge as from the isles of
Javanim,
Crying, "Who now is left upon
the earth
Like him to teach the right and
smite the wrong?"
And from the East, far o'er the
Syrian waste,
Came slowlier, sadlier, the
answering dirge:
"No prophet like him lives or
shall arise
In Israel or the world for
evermore."

But Israel waited, looking
toward the mount,

Till with the deepening eve the
elders came
Saying, "His burial is hid with
God.
We stood far off and saw the
angels lift
His corpse aloft until they
seemed a star
That burnt itself away within the
sky."

The people answered with mute
orphaned gaze
Looking for what had vanished
evermore.
Then through the gloom
without them and within
The spirit's shaping light,
mysterious speech,
Invisible Will wrought clear in
sculptured sound,
The thought-begotten daughter
of the voice,

Thrilled on their listening sense:
"He has no tomb.
He dwells not with you dead,
but lives as Law."

Agatha

Come with me to the mountain,
not where rocks
Soar harsh above the troops of
hurrying pines,
But where the earth spreads
soft and rounded breasts
To feed her children; where the
generous hills
Lift a green isle betwixt the sky
and plain
To keep some Old World things
aloof from change.
Here too 'tis hill and hollow:
new-born streams
With sweet enforcement,
joyously compelled
Like laughing children, hurry
down the steeps,
And make a dimpled chase
athwart the stones;

Pine woods are black upon the
heights, the slopes
Are green with pasture, and the
bearded corn
Fringes the blue above the
sudden ridge:
A little world whose round
horizon cuts
This isle of hills with heaven for
a sea,
Save in clear moments when
southwestward gleams
France by the Rhine, melting
anon to haze.
The monks of old chose here
their still retreat,
And called it by the Blessed
Virgin's name,
Sancta Maria, which the
peasant's tongue,
Speaking from out the parent's
heart that turns
All loved things into little things,

has made
Sanct Märgen, — Holy little
Mary, dear
As all the sweet home things
she smiles upon,
The children and the cows, the
apple-trees,
The cart, the plough, all named
with that caress
Which feigns them little, easy to
be held,
Familiar to the eyes and hand
and heart.
What though a Queen? She puts
her crown away
And with her little Boy wears
common clothes,
Caring for common wants,
remembering
That day when good Saint
Joseph left his work
To marry her with humble trust
sublime.

The monks are gone, their
shadows fall no more
Tall-frocked and cowled athwart
the evening fields
At milking-time; their silent
corridors
Are turned to homes of bare-
armed, aproned men,
Who toil for wife and children.
But the bells,
Pealing on high from two quaint
convent towers,
Still ring the Catholic signals,
summoning
To grave remembrance of the
larger life
That bears our own, like
perishable fruit
Upon its heaven-wide branches.
At their sound
The shepherd boy far off upon
the hill,
The workers with the saw and at

the forge,
The triple generation round the
hearth, —
Grandames and mothers and
the flute-voiced girls, —
Fall on their knees and send
forth prayerful cries
To the kind Mother with the
little Boy,
Who pleads for helpless men
against the storm,
Lightning and plagues and all
terrific shapes
Of power supreme.
Within the prettiest hollow of
these hills,
Just as you enter it, upon the
slope
Stands a low cottage
neighboured cheerily
By running water, which, at
farthest end
Of the same hollow, turns a

heavy mill,
And feeds the pasture for the
miller's cows,
Blanchi and Nägeli, Veilchen and
the rest,
Matrons with faces as Griselda
mild,
Coming at call. And on the
farthest height
A little tower looks out above
the pines
Where mounting you will find a
sanctuary
Open and still; without, the
silent crowd
Of heaven-planted, incense-
mingling flowers;
Within, the altar where the
Mother sits
'Mid votive tablets hung from
far-off years
By peasants succoured in the
peril of fire,

Fever, or flood, who thought
that Mary's love,
Willing but not omnipotent, had
stood
Between their lives and that
dread power which slew
Their neighbour at their side.
The chapel bell
Will melt to gentlest music ere it
reach
That cottage on the slope,
whose garden gate
Has caught the rose-tree boughs
and stands ajar;
So does the door, to let the
sunbeams in;
For in the slanting sunbeams
angels come
And visit Agatha who dwells
within, —
Old Agatha, whose cousins Kate
and Nell
Are housed by her in Love and

Duty's name,
They being feeble, with small
withered wits,
And she believing that the
higher gift
Was given to be shared. So
Agatha
Shares her one room, all neat on
afternoons,
As if some memory were sacred
there
And everything within the four
low walls
An honoured relic.
One long summer's day
An angel entered at the rose-
hung gate,
With skirts pale blue, a brow to
quench the pearl,
Hair soft and blonde as infants',
plenteous
As hers who made the wavy
lengths once speak

The grateful worship of a
rescued soul.
The angel paused before the
open door
To give good day. " Come in, "
said Agatha.
I followed close, and watched
and listened there.
The angel was a lady, noble,
young,
Taught in all seemliness that fits
a court,
All lore that shapes the mind to
delicate use,
Yet quiet, lowly, as a meek
white dove
That with its presence teaches
gentleness.
Men called her Countess Linda;
little girls
In Freiburg town, orphans
whom she caressed,
Said Mamma Linda: yet her

years were few,
Her outward beauties all in
budding time,
Her virtues the aroma of the
plant
That dwells in all its being, root,
stem, leaf,
And waits not ripeness.
" Sit, " said Agatha.
Her cousins were at work in
neighbouring homes
But yet she was not lonely; all
things round
Seemed filled with noiseless yet
responsive life,
As of a child at breast that
gently clings:
Not sunlight only or the
breathing flowers
Or the swift shadows of the
birds and bees,
But all the household goods,
which, polished fair

By hands that cherished them
for service done,
Shone as with glad content. The
wooden beams
Dark and yet friendly, easy to be
reached,
Bore three white crosses for a
speaking sign;
The walls had little pictures
hung a-row,
Telling the stories of Saint
Ursula,
And Saint Elizabeth, the lowly
queen;
And on the bench that served
for table too,
Skirting the wall to save the
narrow space,
There lay the Catholic books,
inherited
From those old times when
printing still was young
With stout-limbed promise, like

a sturdy boy.
And in the farthest corner stood
the bed
Where o'er the pillow hung two
pictures wreathed
With fresh-plucked ivy: one the
Virgin's death,
And one her flowering tomb,
while high above
She smiling bends and lets her
girdle down
For ladder to the soul that
cannot trust
In life which outlasts burial.
Agatha
Sat at her knitting, aged,
upright, slim,
And spoke her welcome with
mild dignity.
She kept the company of kings
and queens
And mitred saints who sat
below the feet

Of Francis with the ragged frock
and wounds;
And Rank for her meant Duty,
various,
Yet equal in its worth, done
worthily.
Command was service;
humblest service done
By willing and discerning souls
was glory.
Fair Countess Linda sat upon the
bench,
Close fronting the old knitter,
and they talked
With sweet antiphony of young
and old.

A GATHA . You like our valley,
lady? I am glad
You thought it well to come
again. But rest —
The walk is long from Master
Michael's inn.

Countess L INDA . Yes, but no
walk is prettier.

A GATHA . It is true:
There lacks no blessing here, the
waters all
Have virtues like the garments
of the Lord,
And heal much sickness; then,
the crops and cows
Flourish past speaking, and the
garden flowers,
Pink, blue, and purple, 'tis a joy
to see
How they yield honey for the
singing bees.
I would the whole world were as
good a home.

Countess L INDA .
And you are well off, Agatha? —
your friends

Left you a certain bread: is it not so?

A GATHA . Not so at all, dear lady. I had nought,
Was a poor orphan; but I came to tend
Here in this house, an old afflicted pair,
Who wore out slowly; and the last who died,
Full thirty years ago, left me this roof
And all the household stuff. It was great wealth;
And so I had a home for Kate and Nell.

Countess L INDA .
But how, then, have you earned your daily bread
These thirty years?

A GATHA . O, that is easy earning.
We help the neighbours, and our bit and sup
Is never failing: they have work for us
In house and field, all sorts of odds and ends,
Patching and mending, turning o'er the hay,
Holding sick children, — there is always work;
And they are very good, — the neighbours are:
Weigh not our bits of work with weight and scale,
But glad themselves with giving us good shares
Of meat and drink; and in the big farm-house
When cloth comes home from weaving, the good wife
Cuts me a piece, — this very

gown, — and says:
" Here, Agatha, you old maid,
you have time
To pray for Hans who is gone
soldiering:
The saints might help him, and
they have much to do,
'Twere well they were besought
to think of him. "
She spoke half jesting, but I
pray, I pray
For poor young Hans. I take it
much to heart
That other people are worse off
than I, —
I ease my soul with praying for
them all.

Countess L INDA . That is your
way of singing, Agatha;
Just as the nightingales pour
forth sad songs,
And when they reach men's ears

they make men's hearts
Feel the more kindly.

A GATHA . Nay, I cannot sing:
My voice is hoarse, and oft I
think my prayers
Are foolish, feeble things; for
Christ is good
Whether I pray or not, — the
Virgin's heart
Is kinder far than mine; and
then I stop
And feel I can do nought
towards helping men,
Till out it comes, like tears that
will not hold,
And I must pray again for all the
world.
'Tis good to me, — I mean the
neighbours are:
To Kate and Nell too. I have
money saved
To go on pilgrimage the second

time.

Countess L INDA . And do you mean to go on pilgrimage
With all your years to carry, Agatha?

A GATHA . The years are light, dear lady: 'tis my sins
Are heavier than I would. And I shall go
All the way to Einsiedeln with that load:
I need to work it off:

Countess L INDA . What sort of sins,
Dear Agatha? I think they must be small.

A GATHA . Nay, but they may be greater than I know;
'Tis but dim light I see by. So I

try
All ways I know of to be
cleansed and pure.
I would not sink where evil
spirits are.
There's perfect goodness
somewhere: so I strive.

Countess L INDA . You were the
better for that pilgrimage
You made before? The shrine is
beautiful;
And then you saw fresh country
all the way.

A GATHA . Yes, that is true. And
ever since that time
The world seems greater, and
the Holy Church
More wonderful. The blessed
pictures all,
The heavenly images with books
and wings,

Are company to me through the
day and night.
The time! the time! It never
seemed far back,
Only to father's father and his
kin
That lived before him. But the
time stretched out
After that pilgrimage: I seemed
to see
Far back, and yet I knew time
lay behind,
As there are countries lying still
behind
The highest mountains, there in
Switzerland.
O, it is great to go on
pilgrimage!

Countess L INDA .
Perhaps some neighbours will
be pilgrims too,
And you can start together in a

band.

A GATHA . Not from these hills:
people are busy here,
The beasts want tendance. One
who is not missed
Can go and pray for others who
must work.
I owe it to all neighbours, young
and old;
For they are good past thinking,
— lads and girls
Given to mischief, merry
naughtiness,
Quiet it, as the hedgehogs
smooth their spines,
For fear of hurting poor old
Agatha.
'Tis pretty: why, the cherubs in
the sky
Look young and merry, and the
angels play
On citherns, lutes, and all sweet

instruments.
I would have young things
merry. See the Lord!
A little baby playing with the
birds;
And how the Blessed Mother
smiles at him.

Countess L INDA . I think you are
too happy, Agatha,
To care for heaven. Earth
contents you well.

A GATHA . Nay, nay, I shall be
called, and I shall go
Right willingly. I shall get
helpless, blind,
Be like an old stalk to be plucked
away:
The garden must be cleared for
young spring plants.
'Tis home beyond the grave, the
most are there,

All those we pray to, all the
Church's lights, —
And poor old souls are welcome
in their rags:
One sees it by the pictures.
Good Saint Ann,
The Virgin's mother, she is very
old,
And had her troubles with her
husband too.
Poor Kate and Nell are younger
far than I,
But they will have this roof to
cover them.
I shall go willingly; and
willingness
Makes the yoke easy and the
burden light.

Countess L INDA .
When you go southward in your
pilgrimage,
Come to see me in Freiburg,

Agatha.
Where you have friends you
should not go to inns.

A GATHA . Yes, I will gladly come
to see you, lady.
And you will give me sweet hay
for a bed,
And in the morning I shall wake
betimes
And start when all the birds
begin to sing.

Countess L INDA .
You wear your smart clothes on
the pilgrimage,
Such pretty clothes as all the
women here
Keep by them for their best: a
velvet cap
And collar golden-broidered?
They look well
On old and young alike.

A GATHA . Nay, I have none, —
Never had better clothes than
these you see.
Good clothes are pretty, but one
sees them best
When others wear them, and I
somehow thought
'Twas not worth while. I had so
many things
More than some neighbours, I
was partly shy
Of wearing better clothes than
they, and now
I am so old and custom is so
strong
'Twould hurt me sore to put on
finery.

Countess L INDA . Your grey hair
is a crown, dear Agatha.
Shake hands; good-bye. The sun
is going down,

And I must see the glory from
the hill.

I stayed among those hills; and
oft heard more
Of Agatha. I liked to hear her
name,
As that of one half grandame
and half saint,
Uttered with reverent
playfulness. The lads
And younger men all called her
mother, aunt,
Or granny, with their pet
diminutives,
And bade their lasses and their
brides behave
Right well to one who surely
made a link
'Twixt faulty folk and God by
loving both:
Not one but counted service
done by her,

Asking no pay save just her daily
bread.
At feasts and weddings, when
they passed in groups
Along the vale, and the good
country wine,
Being vocal in them, made them
quire along
In quaintly mingled mirth and
piety,
They fain must jest and play
some friendly trick
On three old maids; but when
the moment came
Always they bated breath and
made their sport
Gentle as feather-stroke, that
Agatha
Might like the waking for the
love it showed.
Their song made happy music
'mid the hills,
For nature tuned their race to

harmony,
And poet Hans, the tailor, wrote
them songs
That grew from out their life, as
crocuses
From out the meadow's
moistness. 'Twas his song
They oft sang, wending
homeward from a feast, —
The song I give you. It brings in,
you see,
Their gentle jesting with the
three old maids.

Midnight by the chapel bell!
Homeward, homeward all,
farewell!
I with you, and you with me,
Miles are short with company.
Heart of Mary, bless the way ,
Keep us all by night and day!

Moon and stars at feast with

night
Now have drunk their fill of
light.
Home they hurry, making time
Trot apace, like merry rhyme.
Heart of Mary, mystic rose ,
Send us all a sweet repose!

Swiftly through the wood down
hill,
Run till you can hear the mill.
Toni's ghost is wandering now,
Shaped just like a snow-white
cow.
Heart of Mary, morning star ,
Ward off danger, near or far!

Toni's waggon with its load
Fell and crushed him in the
road
'Twixt these pine-trees. Never
fear!
Give a neighbour's ghost good

cheer.
Holy Babe, our God and Brother
,
Bind us fast to one another!

Hark! the mill is at its work,
Now we pass beyond the murk
To the hollow, where the moon
Makes her silvery afternoon.
Good Saint Joseph, faithful
spouse ,
Help us all to keep our vows!

Here the three old maidens
dwell,
Agatha and Kate and Nell;
See, the moon shines on the
thatch,
We will go and shake the latch.
Heart of Mary, cup of joy ,
Give us mirth without alloy!

Hush, 'tis here, no noise, sing

low,
Rap with gentle knuckles — so!
Like the little tapping birds,
On the door; then sing good
words.
Meek Saint Anna, old and fair ,
Hallow all the snow-white hair!

Little maidens old, sweet
dreams!
Sleep one sleep till morning
beams.
Mothers ye, who help us all,
Quick at hand, if ill befall.
Holy Gabriel, lily-laden ,
Bless the aged mother-maiden!

Forward, mount the broad
hillside
Swift as soldiers when they
ride.
See the two towers how they
peep,

Round-capped giants, o'er the
steep.
Heart of Mary, by thy sorrow ,
Keep us upright through the
morrow!

Now they rise quite suddenly
Like a man from bended knee,
Now Saint Märgen is in sight,
Here the roads branch off —
good night!
Heart of Mary, by thy grace ,
Give us with the saints a place!

"It is never too late to be
what you might have been."

-    George Eliot

Above: George Eliot's Signature

Mary Ann Evans, aka George Eliot (1819 – 1880)

Portrait by Samuel Laurence, 1860